VICTORIAN
LOVE POEMS

A. Norman Jeffares was born in Dublin and now lives at Fife Ness in Scotland. He has held several professorships and published many books including *A History of Anglo-Irish Literature* (1982), *W. B. Yeats: A New Biography* (1988), *Yeats: The Love Poems* (1990) and *Swift: The Selected Poems* (1992). With Brendan Kennelly he has edited *James Joyce: The Poems, Verse and Prose* (1992) and, with Brendan Kennelly and Katie Donovan, *Ireland's Women: Writings Past and Present* (1994). His *W. B. Yeats: Man and Poet* has been reissued in a third edition (1996) by Kyle Cathie Limited, and his most recent book is *Images of Invention*, a collection of his essays on Irish writing. He is at present editing *The Letters of Iseult Gonne to W. B. Yeats* with Christina Bridgwater and Anna White, with whom he edited *Always Your Friend: The Gonne-Yeats Letters* (1992).

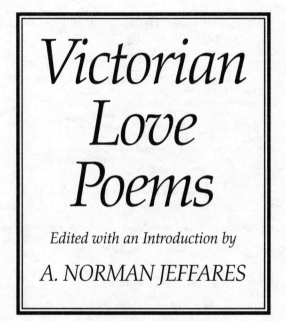

Victorian Love Poems

Edited with an Introduction by

A. NORMAN JEFFARES

KYLE CATHIE LIMITED

To Jeanne

First published in Great Britain in 1996 by
Kyle Cathie Limited
20 Vauxhall Bridge Road, London SW1V 2SA

ISBN 1 85626 242 1

Selection, Introduction and Notes
copyright ©A. Norman Jeffares 1997

A. Norman Jeffares is hereby identified as the Editor of
this work in accordance with Section 77 of the
Copyright, Designs and Patents Act 1988.

A Cataloguing in Publication record for this title is
available from the British Library.

Typeset by SX Composing DTP, Rayleigh, Essex
Printed by Cox & Wyman Ltd, Reading

Contents

INTRODUCTION

The range of Victorian love poetry is striking: the excitement of love at first sight, its joy and delight, the increase of affection, the pain of rejection or separation or desertion, the effects of envy or jealousy or suspicion, the close interweaving of personalities in marriage, the desolation dealt out by the death of a lover, a mistress, a husband or a wife.

All these we might expect from poets of imagination and sensitivity whose beings were attuned to the emotional impact of others on them and their own impact on others, but there were other elements shaping the love poems of the Victorians. The peace of the age and its industrial, scientific progress, its imperial power and influence allowed them a certain ease in the development of their theme. Consequently they often wrote somewhat lengthy love poems. But there was an unease as well. They did not escape the strains scientific thought imposed upon their religious belief, nor those occasioned by the increasing incertitude of women about the institution of marriage – when the dice were so loaded in favour of men – and the insistence of many women on intellectual independence. And there was an awareness of the fragility of human life, a very Victorian sense of the imminence of death.

Many currents ran together in Victorian love poetry. There was a strong romantic element in it. Romantic relationships between men ranged from close friendships (of the kind, for instance, that fuelled *In Memoriam*) and the homosexuality of which Wilde became the age's outstanding example. Women developed romantic friendships with other women with similar variations in intensity. And George Eliot's deep attachment to her brother reminds us of the variety of relationships that the word love can convey.

Victorian romance could sometimes decline into sentimentality. The dramatic could slide off into the declamatory – as the Brownings demonstrate. The confessional could convert into lamentation, at times verging upon the lachrymose. The challenging voice could comfortably change into the celebratory. The gamut of human emotions is there in these poems: sometimes the confession is raw, sometimes refined, sometimes intellectualised, sometimes inhibited. The tones include the ironic, the comic, the witty, the deprecating, the doubting (Clough is a master of this). Sometimes there is an honest recording of a failure of nerve, as in Arnold's case; sometimes a poet traces the break-up of a relationship, something Meredith does devastatingly in 'Modern Love'. Victorian love poetry is outspoken, then, and perhaps more so than is generally allowed. As well as being profoundly serious on the one hand, sometimes superficially sentimental on the other, its conventions and codes convey an enjoyable wealth of human experience: emotional, intellectual, sensuous and even sexual.

The poets had their audience in mind as they wrote, so their poetry reads very well aloud. The level of technical competence was very high and so there are many memorable lines in this anthology which may seem familiar: they owe their survival to a mastery of rhyme and rhythm as well as arresting thought or imagery. The work of lesser-known poets is, however, included for many of the minor poets produced evocative, effective and original poems, often independent of current fashions. The poets chosen are English, Scottish, Welsh and Irish.

As the nineteenth century progressed poetry inevitably changed. High romance gave way to rhetoric, such as we find in the attack of Dante Gabriel Rossetti's opening lines, and to increasing realism, a natural evolution well expressed in Yeats's 'Adam's Curse'. Victorian is here defined as poetry written by those poets born after Victoria's accession in 1837 and before her death in 1901.

Rather than employ an orthodox chronological presentation however, or a grouping together of individual poets' poems, or a distribution of all the poems selected into themes or categories, this anthology presents the poems in the alphabetical order of the first words of their opening lines. This arrangement (with its sometimes surprising juxtapositions) has been adopted in order to convey the sheer variety, the compelling power and rich complexity, indeed the impressive achievement of Victorian love poetry.

A. Norman Jeffares
Fife Ness, 1996

ACKNOWLEDGEMENTS

I am particularly grateful to Colin Smythe for providing an unpublished poem by Lady Gregory and to Peter van de Kamp for providing two unpublished poems by Katharine Tynan.

The Phantom Wooer

A ghost, that loved a lady fair,
Ever in the starry air
Of midnight at her pillow stood;
And, with a sweetness skies above
The luring words of human love,
Her soul the phantom wooed.
Sweet and sweet is their poisoned note,
The little snakes of silver throat,
In mossy skulls that nest and lie,
Ever singing, 'Die, oh! die.'

Young soul put off your flesh, and come
With me into the quiet tomb,
Our bed is lovely, dark and sweet;
The earth will swing us, as she goes,
Beneath our coverlid of snows,
And the warm leaden sheet.
Dear and dear is their poisoned note,
The little snakes of silver throat,
In mossy skulls that nest and lie,
Ever singing, 'Die, oh! die.'

Thomas Lovell Beddoes

A May Song

A little while my love and I
Before the mowing of the hay,
Twined daisy-chains and cowslip balls,
And carolled glees and madrigals,
Before the hay, beneath the may,
My love (who loved me then) and I.

For long years now my love and I
Tread severed paths to varied ends;
We sometimes meet, and sometimes say
The trivial things of every day,
And meet as comrades, meet as friends,
My love (who loved me once) and I.

But never more my love and I
Will wander forth, as once, together,
Or sing the songs we used to sing
In spring-time, in the cloudless weather;
Some chord is mute that used to ring,
Some word forgot we used to say
Amongst the may, before the hay,
My love (who loves me not) and I.

Mary Montgomerie, Lady Currie

My Marriage-Morn

Across the sky the daylight crept,
And birds grew garrulous in the grove,
And on my marriage-morn I slept
A soft sleep, undisturbed by love.

Coventry Patmore

Meeting

Again I see my bliss at hand,
The town, the lake are here;
My Marguerite smiles upon the strand,
Unaltered with the year.

I know that graceful figure fair,
That cheek of languid hue;
I know that soft, enkerchiefed hair,
And those sweet eyes of blue.

Again I spring to make my choice;
Again in tones of ire
I hear a God's tremendous voice:
'Be counselled, and retire.'

Ye guiding Powers who join and part,
What would ye have with me?
Ah, warn some more ambitious heart,
And let the peaceful be!

Matthew Arnold

A Pure Hypothesis

A Lover, in Four-dimensioned Space, describes a Dream

Ah, love, the teacher we decried,
That erudite professor grim,
In mathematics drenched and dyed,
Too hastily we scouted him.
He said: 'The bounds of Time and Space,
The categories we revere,
May be in quite another case
In quite another sphere.'

He told us: 'Science can conceive
A race whose feeble comprehension
Can't be persuaded to believe
That there exists our Fourth Dimension,
Whom Time and Space for ever baulk;
But of these beings incomplete,
Whether upon their heads they walk
Or stand upon their feet –

We cannot tell, we do not know,
Imagination stops confounded;
We can but say "It *may* be so,"
To every theory propounded,'
Too glad were we in this our scheme
Of things, his notions to embrace, –
But – I have dreamed an awful dream
of *Three-dimensioned* Space!

I dreamed – the horror seemed to stun
My logical perception strong,
That everything beneath the sun
Was *so unutterably wrong.*
I thought – what words can I command? –
That nothing ever did come right.
No wonder *you* can't understand:
I could not, till last night!

I would not, if I could, recall
The horror of those novel heavens,
Where Present, Past, and Future all
Appeared at sixes and at sevens,
Where Capital and Labour fought,
And, in the nightmare of the mind,
No contradictories were thought
As truthfully combined!

Nay, in that dream-distorted clime,
These fatal wilds I wandered through,
The boundaries of Space and Time
Had got most frightfully askew.
'What is "askew"?' my love, you cry;
I cannot answer, can't portray;
The sense of Everything awry
No language can convey.

I can't tell what my words denote,
I know not what my phrases mean:
Inexplicable terrors float
Before this spirit once serene.
Ah, what if on some lurid star
There should exist a hapless race,
Who live and love, who think and are,
In Three-dimensioned Space!

May Kendall

Ah, My Own Dear One Do Not Leave Me Yet

(From A Woman's Sonnets II)

Ah, my own dear one do not leave me yet!
Let me a little longer hold thy hand.
It is too soon to ask me to forget
Too soon I should from happiness be banned.
The future holds no hope of good for me,
The past I only wish to shut away
But while thou'rt with me and thy face I see
The sun shines on me, it is always day.
And time and fate bring near our parting hour
Which well I know thy love will not outlast –
But then perchance I may have gained more power
More strength and will to bury my dead past
Ah! try to love me still a moment's space
'Tis all I ask thee dear, this little grace.

Augusta, Lady Gregory

Love Versus Learning

Alas, for the blight of my fancies!
Alas, for the fall of my pride!
I planned, in my girlish romances,
To be a philosopher's bride.

I pictured him learned and witty,
The sage and the lover combined,
Not scorning to say I was pretty,
Nor only adoring my *mind*.

No elderly, spectacled Mentor,
But one who would worship and woo;
Perhaps I might take an inventor,
Or even a poet would do.

And tender and gay and well-favoured,
My fate overtook me at last:
I saw, and I heard, and I wavered,
I smiled, and my freedom was past.

He promised to love me for ever,
He pleaded, and what could I say?
I thought he must surely be clever,
For he is an Oxford M.A.

But now, I begin to discover
My visions are fatally marred;
Perfection itself as a lover,
He's neither a sage nor a bard.

He's mastered the usual knowledge,
And says it's a terrible bore;
He formed his opinions at college,
Then why should he think any more?

My logic he sets at defiance,
Declares that my Latin's no use,
And when I begin to talk Science
He calls me a dear little goose.

He says that my lips are too rosy
To speak in a language that's dead,
And all that is dismal and prosy
Should fly from so sunny a head.

He scoffs at each grave occupation,
Turns everything off with a pun;
And says that his sole calculation
Is how to make two into one.

He says Mathematics may vary,
Geometry cease to be true,
But scorning the slightest vagary
He still will continue to woo.

He says that the sun may stop action,
But he will not swerve from his course;
For love is his law of attraction,
A smile his centripetal force.

His levity's truly terrific,
And often I think we must part,
But compliments so scientific
Recapture my fluttering heart.

Yet sometimes 'tis very confusing,
This conflict of love and of lore –
But hark! I must cease from my musing,
For that is his knock at the door!

Constance Naden

The Lover Tells of the Rose in his Heart

All things uncomely and broken, all things worn out
    and old,
The cry of a child by the roadway, the creak of a
    lumbering cart,
The heavy steps of the ploughman, splashing the wintry
    mould,
Are wronging your image that blossoms a rose in the
    deeps of my heart.

The wrong of unshapely things is a wrong too great to
    be told;
I hunger to build them anew and sit on a green knoll
    apart,
With the earth and the sky and the water, re-made, like
    a casket of gold
For my dreams of your image that blossoms a rose in
    the deeps of my heart.

W. B. Yeats

Amo, Amas

Amo, Amas, I love a lass
As a cedar tall and slender;
Sweet cowslip's grace is her nominative case,
And she's of the feminine gender.

Rorum, Corum, sunt divorum,
Harum, Scarum divo;
Tag-rag, merry-derry, periwig and hat-band
Hic hoc horum genitivo.

Can I decline a Nymph divine?
Her voice as a flute is dulcis,
Her oculus bright, her manus white,
And soft, when I tacto, her pulse is.

Rorum, Corum, sunt divorum,
Harum, Scarum divo;
Tag-rag, merry-derry, periwig and hat-band
Hic hoc horum genitivo.

Oh, how bella my puella,
I'll kiss secula seculorum.
If I've luck, sir, she's my uxor,
O dies benedictorum.

Rorum, Corum, sunt divorum,
Harum, Scarum divo;
Tag-rag, merry-derry, periwig and hat-band
Hic hoc horum genitivo.

John O'Keefe

Annie She's Dowie

Annie she's dowie, and Willie he's wae:
What can be the matter wi' siccan a twae,
For Annie she's fair as the first o' the day,
And Willie he's honest and stalwart and gay?

Oh, the tane has a daddy is poor and is proud,
And the tither a minnie that cleiks at the goud!
They lo'ed ane anither, and said their say,
But the daddy and minnie hae partit the twae!

George MacDonald

At Castle Boterel

As I drive to the junction of lane and highway,
And the drizzle bedrenches the waggonette,
I look behind at the fading byway,
And see on its slope, now glistening wet,
Distinctly yet

Myself and a girlish form benighted
In dry March weather. We climb the road
Beside a chaise. We had just alighted
To ease the sturdy pony's load
When he sighed and slowed.

What we did as we climbed, and what we talked of
Matters not much, nor to what it led, –
Something that life will not be balked of
Without rude reason till hope is dead,
And feeling fled.

It filled but a minute. But was there ever
A time of such quality, since or before,
In that hill's story? To one mind never,
Though it has been climbed, foot-swift, foot-sore,
By thousands more.

Primeaval rocks form the road's steep border,
And much have they faced there, first and last,
Of the transitory in Earth's long order;
But what they record in colour and cast
Is – that we two passed.

And to me, though Time's unflinching rigour,
In mindless rote, has ruled from sight
The substance now, one phantom figure
Remains on the slope, as when that night
Saw us alight.

I look and see it there, shrinking, shrinking,
I look back at it amid the rain
For the very last time; for my sand is sinking,
And I shall traverse old love's domain
Never again.

Thomas Hardy

My Love's Guardian Angel

As in the cool-aïred road I come by,
– in the night,
Under the moon-climed height o' the sky,
– in the night,
There by the lime's broad lim's as I did stäy,
While in the air dark sheädes wer' at plaÿ
Up on the windor-glass that did keep
Lew vrom the wind, my true love asleep,
– in the night.

While in the grey-walled height o' the tow'r,
– in the night,
Sounded the midnight bell wi' the hour,
– in the night,
There come a bright heäired angel that shed
Light vrom her white robe's zilvery thread,
Wi' her vore-vinger held up to meäke
Silence around lest sleepers mid weäke,
– in the night.

'Oh! then,' I whispered, 'do I behold
– in the night.
Linda, my true-love, here in the cwold in the night?'
'No,' she meäde answer, 'you do misteäke:
She is asleep, 'tis I be aweäke;
I be her angel brightly a-drest,
Watchèn her slumber while she do rest,
– in the night.'

'Zee how the clear win's, brisk in the bough,
– in the night,
While they do pass, don't smite on her brow,
– in the night;
Zee how the cloud-sheädes naïseless do zweep
Over the house-top where she's asleep.
You, too, goo on, though times mid be near,
When you, wi' me, mid speäk to her ear
– in the night.'

William Barnes

The Visiting Sea

As the unhastening tide doth roll,
Home from the deep, along the whole
Wide shining strand, and floods the caves,
– Your love comes filling with happy waves
The open sea-shore of my soul.

But inward from the seaward spaces,
None knows, not even you, the places
Brimmed, at your coming, out of sight,
– The little solitudes of delight
The tide constrains in dim embraces.

You see the happy shore, wave-rimmed,
But know not of the quiet dimmed
Rivers your coming floods and fills,
The little pools 'mid happier hills,
My silent rivulets, over-brimmed.

What! I have secrets from you? Yes,
But, visiting sea, your love doth press
And reach in further than you know,
And fills all these; and, when you go,
There's loneliness in loneliness.

Alice Meynell

Lost On Both Sides

(From The House of Life – Sonnet XCI)

As when two men have loved a woman well,
Each hating each, through Love's and Death's deceit;
Since not for either this stark marriage-sheet
And the long pauses of this wedding-bell;
Yet o'er her grave the night and day dispel
At last their feud forlorn, with cold and heat;
Nor other than dear friends to death may fleet
The two lives left that most of her can tell:–

So separate hopes, which in a soul had wooed
The one same Peace, strove with each other long,
And Peace before their faces perished since:
So through that soul, in restless brotherhood,
They roam together now, and wind among
Its bye-streets, knocking at the dusty inns.

Dante Gabriel Rossetti

Ask Me No More

(From The Princess)

Ask me no more: the moon may draw the sea;
The cloud may stoop from heaven and take the shape
With fold to fold, of mountain or of cape;
But O too fond, when have I answered thee?
Ask me no more.

Ask me no more: what answer should I give?
I love not hollow cheek or faded eye:
Yet, O my friend, I will not have thee die!
Ask me no more, lest I should bid thee live;
Ask me no more.

Ask me no more: thy fate and mine are sealed,
I strove against the stream and all in vain;
Let the great river take me to the main:
No more, dear love, for at a touch I yield;
Ask me no more.

Alfred, Lord Tennyson

Masquerading

At dawn she unmasked –
And – oh, heaven! 'twas her sister!
All her love I had asked
Ere at dawn she unmasked;
In her smile I had basked,
I had coyed her, had kissed her –
At dawn she unmasked –
And – oh, heaven! 'twas her sister!

May Probyn

Modern Love XVII

At dinner, she is hostess, I am host,
Went the feast ever cheerfuller? She keeps
The Topic over intellectual deeps
In buoyancy afloat. They see no ghost.
With sparkling surface-eyes we ply the ball;
It is in truth a most contagious game:
HIDING THE SKELETON, shall be its name.
Such play as this the devils might appal!
But here's the greater wonder; in that we,
Enamoured of an acting nought can tire,
Each other, like true hypocrites, admire;
Warm-lighted looks, Love's ephemerioe,
Shoot gaily o'er the dishes and the wine.
We waken envy of our happy lot.
Fast, sweet, and golden, shows the marriage-knot.
Dear guests, you now have seen Love's corpse-light
 shine.

George Meredith

The Dawning Of The Day

At early dawn I once had been
Where Lene's blue waters flow,
When summer bid the groves be green,
The lamp of light to glow.
As on by bower, and town, and tower,
And widespread fields I stray.
I meet a maid in the greenwood shade
At the dawning of the day.

Her feet and beauteous head were bare,
No mantle fair she wore;
But down her waist fell golden hair,

That swept the tall grass o'er.
With milking-pail she sought the vale,
And bright her charms' display;
Outshining far the morning star
At the dawning of the day.

Beside me sat that maid divine
Where grassy banks outspread.
'Oh, let me call thee ever mine,
Dear maid,' I sportive said.
'False man, for shame, why bring me blame?'
She cried, and burst away –
The sun's first light pursued her flight
At the dawning of the day

Edward Walsh

Nuptial Sleep

At length their long kiss severed with sweet smart:
And as the last slow sudden drops are shed
From sparkling eaves when all the storm has fled,
So singly flagged the pulses of each heart.
Their bosoms sundered, with the opening start
Of married flowers to either side outspread
From the knit stem; yet still their mouths, burnt red,
Fawned on each other where they lay apart.

Sleep sank them lower than the tide of dreams,
And their dreams watched them sink, and slid away.
Slowly their souls swam up again, through gleams
Of watered light and dull drowned waifs of day;
Till from some wonder of new woods and streams
He woke, and wondered more. For there she lay.

Dante Gabriel Rossetti

At The Mid Hour Of Night

At the mid hour of night, when stars are weeping, I fly
To the lone vale we loved, when life shone warm in
thine eye;
And I think oft, if spirits can steal from the regions of
air,
To revisit past scenes of delight, thou wilt come to me
there,
And tell me our love is remembered, even in the sky.

Then I sing the wild song 'twas once such pleasure to
hear!
When our voices commingling breathed, like one, on
the ear;
And, as Echo far off through the vale my sad orison
rolls,
I think, O my love! 'tis thy voice from the Kingdom of
Souls,
Faintly answering still the notes that once were so dear.

Thomas Moore

At Her Window

Beating Heart! we come again
Where my Love reposes:
This is Mabel's window-pane;
These are Mabel's roses.

Is she nested? Does she kneel
In the twilight stilly,
Lily clad from throat to heel,
She, my virgin Lily?

Soon the wan, the wistful stars,
Fading, will forsake her;
Elves of light, on beamy bars,
Whisper then, and wake her.

Let this friendly pebble plead
At her flowery grating;
If she hear me will she heed?
Mabel, I am waiting.

Mabel will be decked anon,
Zoned in bride's apparel;
Happy zone! O hark to yon
Passion-shaken carol!

Sing thy song, thou trancèd thrush,
Pipe thy best, thy clearest; –
Hush, her lattice moves, O hush –
Dearest Mabel! – dearest . . .

Frederick Locker-Lampson

Because I liked You Better

Because I liked you better
Than suits a man to say,
It irked you, and I promised
To throw the thought away.

To put the world between us
We parted, stiff and dry;
'Good-bye', said you, 'forget me.'
'I will, no fear', said I.

If here, where clover whitens
The dead man's knoll, you pass,

And no tall flower to meet you
Starts in the trefoiled grass,

Halt by the headstone naming
The heart no longer stirred,
And say the lad that loved you
Was one that kept his word.

A. E. Housman

Alchemy

Because of the light of the moon,
Silver is found on the moor;
And because of the light of the sun,
There is gold on the walls of the poor.

Because of the light of the stars,
Planets are found in the stream;
And because of the light of your eyes
There is love in the depths of my dream.

Francis Carlin

A Woman's Question

Before I trust my Fate to thee,
Or place my hand in thine,
Before I let thy Future give
Colour and form to mine,
Before I peril all for thee, question thy soul to-night for
   me.

I break all slighter bonds, nor feel
A shadow of regret:
Is there one link within the Past,
That holds thy spirit yet?
Or is thy Faith as clear and free as that which I can
pledge to thee?

Does there within thy dimmest dreams
A possible future shine,
Wherein thy life could henceforth breathe,
Untouched, unshared by mine?
If so, at any pain or cost, oh, tell me before all is lost.

Look deeper still. If thou canst feel
Within thy inmost soul,
That thou hast kept a portion back,
While I have staked the whole;
Let no false pity spare the blow, but in true mercy tell
me so.

Is there within thy heart a need
That mine cannot fulfil?
One chord that any other hand
Could better wake or still?
Speak now – lest at some future day my whole life
wither and decay.

Lives there within thy nature hid
The demon-spirit Change,
Shedding a passing glory still
On all things new and strange? –
It may not be thy fault alone – but shield my heart
against thy own.

Couldst thou withdraw thy hand one day
And answer to my claim,
That Fate, and that to-day's mistake,
Not thou – had been to blame?

Some soothe their conscience thus: but thou, wilt surely
   warn and save me now.

Nay, answer *not* – I dare not hear,
The words would come too late;
Yet I would spare thee all remorse,
So, comfort thee, my Fate –
Whatever on my heart may fall – remember, I *would* risk
   it all!

Adelaide Anne Procter

Natura Naturans

Beside me, – in the car, – she sat,
She spake not, no, nor looked to me:
From her to me, from me to her,
What passed so subtly stealthily?
As rose to rose that by it blows
Its interchanged aroma flings;
Or wake to sound of one sweet note
The virtues of disparted strings.

Beside me, nought but this! – but this,
That influent as within me dwelt
Her life, mine too within her breast,
Her brain, her every limb she felt:
We sat; while o'er and in us, more
And more, a power unknown prevailed
Inhaling, and inhaled – and still
'Twas one, inhaling or inhaled.

Beside me, nought but this; – and passed;
I passed; and know not to this day
If gold or jet her girlish hair,
If black, or brown, or lucid-grey

Her eye's young glance: the fickle chance
That joined us, yet may join again;
But I no face again could greet
As hers, whose life was in me then.

Touched not, nor looked; yet owned we both
The Power which e'en in stones and earths
By blind elections felt, in forms
Organic breeds to myriad births;
By lichen small on granite wall
Approved, its faintest feeblest stir
Slow-spreading, strengthening long, at last
Vibrated full in me and her.

In me and her – sensation strange!
The lily grew to pendent head,
To vernal airs the mossy bank
Its sheeny primrose spangles spread,
In roof o'er roof of shade sun-proof
Did cedar strong itself outclimb,
And altitude of aloe proud
Aspire in floreal crown sublime;

Flashed flickering forth fantastic flies,
Big bees their burly bodies swung,
Rooks roused with civic din the elms,
And lark its wild reveillez rung;
In Libyan dell the light gazelle,
The leopard lithe in Indian glade,
And dolphin, brightening tropic seas,
In us were living, leapt and played:

Their shells did slow crustacea build,
Their gilded skins did snakes renew,
While mightier spines for loftier kind
Their types in amplest limbs outgrew;
Yea, close comprest in human breast,
What moss, and tree, and livelier thing,

What Earth, Sun, Star of force possest,
Lay budding, burgeoning forth for Spring.

Such sweet preluding sense of old
Led on in Eden's sinless place
The hour when bodies human first
Combined the primal prime embrace,
Such genial heat the blissful seat
In man and woman owned unblamed,
When, naked both, its garden paths
They walked unconscious, unashamed:

Ere, clouded yet in mistiest dawn,
Above the horizon dusk and dun,
One mountain crest with light had tipped
That Orb that is the Spirit's Sun;
Ere dreamed young flowers in vernal showers
Of fruit to rise the flower above,
Or ever yet to young Desire
Was told of the mystic name of Love.

Arthur Hugh Clough

Amor Profanus
For Gabriel De Lautrec

Beyond the pale of memory,
In some mysterious dusky grove;
A place of shadows utterly,
Where never cooes the turtle-dove,
A world forgotten of the sun:
I dreamed we met when day was done,
And marvelled at our ancient love.

Met there by chance, long kept apart,
We wandered through the darkling glades;

And that old language of the heart
We sought to speak: alas! poor shades!
Over our pallid lips had run
The waters of oblivion,
Which crown all loves of men or maids.

In vain we stammered: from afar
Our old desire shone cold and dead:
That time was distant as a star,
When eyes were bright and lips were red,
And still we went with downcast eye
And no delight in being nigh,
Poor shadows most uncomforted.

Ah, Lalage! while life is ours,
Hoard not thy beauty rose and white,
But pluck the pretty, fleeting flowers
That deck our little path of light:
For all too soon we train shall tread
The bitter pastures of the dead:
Estranged, sad spectres of the night.

Ernest Dowson

Perfection

By Perfection fooled too long,
I will dream of that no longer!
Venus, you have done me wrong
By your unattainable beauty,
Till it seemed to be my duty
To belittle all the throng.
I have found attraction stronger;
I have found a lady younger
Who can make a hard heart stir;
Like an athlete, tall and slender,

With no more than human splendour;
Yet, for all the faults of her,
Than Perfection perfecter.

Though she guards it, grace breaks through
Every blithe and careless movement;
What shall I compare her to?
When she takes the ball left-handed,
Speed and sweetness are so blended
Nothing awkward she can do,
She, whose faults are an improvement!
If she only knew what Love meant
I would not be seeking now
To describe the curbed perfection
Of all loveliness in action –
Perfect she would be, I vow,
With the mole above the brow!

Oliver St John Gogarty

Remembrance

Cold in the earth – and the deep snow piled above thee!
Far, far removed, cold in the dreary grave!
Have I forgot, my only love, to love thee,
Severed at last by time's all-severing wave?

Now, when alone, do my thoughts no longer hover
Over the mountains, on that northern shore,
Resting their wings where heath and fern-leaves cover
Thy noble heart for ever, ever more?

Cold in the earth, and fifteen wild Decembers
From those brown hills have melted into spring:
Faithful indeed is the spirit that remembers
After such years of change and suffering!

Sweet love of youth, forgive if I forget thee
While the world's tide is bearing me along:
Sterner desires and darker hopes beset me,
Hopes which obscure, but cannot do thee wrong!

No later light has lightened up my heaven,
No second morn has ever shone for me;
All my life's bliss from thy dear life was given,
All my life's bliss is in the grave with thee.

But when the days of golden dreams had perished,
And even despair was powerless to destroy,
Then did I learn how existence could be cherished,
Strengthened and fed without the aid of joy.

Then did I check the tears of useless passion –
Weaned my young soul from yearning after thine;
Sternly denied its burning wish to hasten
Down to that tomb already more than mine.

And, even yet, I dare not let it languish,
Dare not indulge in memory's rapturous pain;
Once drinking deep of that divinest anguish,
How could I seek the empty world again?

Emily Brontë

And On My Eyes Dark Sleep By Night

Come, dark-eyed sleep, thou child of night,
Give me thy dreams, thy lies;
Lead through the horny portal white
The pleasure day denies.

O bring the kiss I could not take
From lips that would not give;

Bring me the heart I could not break,
The bliss for which I live.

I care not if I slumber blest
By fond delusion; nay,
Put me on Phaon's lips to rest,
And cheat the cruel day!

Michael Field

Come Down, O Maid

(From The Princess)

Come down, O maid, from yonder mountain height:
What pleasure lives in height (the shepherd sang),
In height and cold, the splendour of the hills?
But cease to move so near the Heavens, and cease
To glide a sunbeam by the blasted Pine,
To sit a star upon the sparkling spire;
And come, for Love is of the valley, come,
For Love is of the valley, come thou down
And find him; by the happy threshold, he,
Or hand in hand with Plenty in the maize,
Or red with spirted purple of the vats,
Or foxlike in the vine; nor cares to walk
With Death and Morning on the silver horns,
Nor wilt thou snare him in the white ravine,
Nor find him dropt upon the firths of ice,
That huddling slant in furrow-cloven falls
To roll the torrent out of dusky doors:
But follow; let the torrent dance thee down
To find him in the valley; let the wild
Lean-headed Eagles yelp alone, and leave
The monstrous ledges there to slope, and spill
Their thousand wreaths of dangling water-smoke,
That like a broken purpose waste in air:

So waste not thou; but come; for all the vales
Await thee; azure pillars of the hearth
Arise to thee; the children call, and I
Thy shepherd pipe, and sweet is every sound,
Sweeter thy voice, but every sound is sweet;
Myriads of rivulets hurrying through the lawn,
The moan of doves in immemorial elms,
And murmuring of innumerable bees.

Alfred, Lord Tennyson

From **Maud**
(Part 1, XXII)

Come into the garden, Maud,
For the black bat, night, has flown,
Come into the garden, Maud,
I am here at the gate alone;
And the woodbine spices are wafted abroad,
And the musk of the roses blown.

For a breeze of morning moves,
And the planet of Love is on high,
Beginning to faint in the light that she loves
On a bed of daffodil sky,
To faint in the light of the sun she loves,
To faint in his light, and to die.

All night have the roses heard
The flute, violin, bassoon;
All night has the casement jessamine stirred
To the dancers dancing in tune;
Till a silence fell with the waking bird,
And a hush with the setting moon.

I said to the lily, 'There is but one
With whom she has heart to be gay.
When will the dancers leave her alone?
She is weary of dance and play.'
Now half to the setting moon are gone,
And half to the rising day;
Low on the sand and loud on the stone
The last wheel echoes away.

I said to the rose, 'The brief night goes
In babble and revel and wine.
O young lord-lover, what sighs are those,
For one that will never be thine?
But mine, but mine,' so I sware to the rose,
'For ever and ever, mine.'

And the soul of the rose went into my blood,
As the music clashed in the hall;
And long by the garden lake I stood,
For I heard your rivulet fall
From the lake to the meadow and on to the wood,
Our wood, that is dearer than all;

From the meadow your walks have left so sweet
That whenever a March-wind sighs
He sets the jewel-print of your feet
In violets blue as your eyes,
To the woody hollows in which we meet
And the valleys of Paradise.

The slender acacia would not shake
One long milk-bloom on the tree;
The white lake-blossom fell into the lake,
As the pimpernel dozed on the lea;
But the rose was awake all night for your sake,
Knowing your promise to me;
The lilies and roses were all awake,
They sighed for the dawn and thee.

Queen rose of the rosebud garden of girls,
Come hither, the dances are done,
In gloss of satin and glimmer of pearls,
Queen lily and rose in one;
Shine out, little head, sunning over with curls,
To the flowers, and be their sun.

There has fallen a splendid tear
From the passion-flower at the gate.
She is coming, my dove, my dear;
She is coming, my life, my fate;
The red rose cries, 'She is near, she is near;'
And the white rose weeps, 'She is late;'
The larkspur listens, 'I hear, I hear;'
And the lily whispers, 'I wait.'

She is coming, my own, my sweet;
Were it ever so airy a tread,
My heart would hear her and beat,
Were it earth in an earthy bed;
My dust would hear her and beat,
Had I lain for a century dead;
Would start and tremble under her feet,
And blossom in purple and red.

Alfred, Lord Tennyson

Come Not, When I Am Dead

Come not, when I am dead,
To drop thy foolish tears upon my grave,
To trample round my fallen head,
And vex the unhappy dust thou wouldst not save.
There let the wind sweep and the plover cry;
But thou, go by.

Child, if it were thine error or thy crime
I care no longer, being all unblest:
Wed whom thou wilt, but I am sick of Time,
And I desire to rest.
Pass on, weak heart, and leave me where I lie;
Go by, go by.

Alfred, Lord Tennyson

From Silent Is The House

Come, the wind may never again
Blow as now it blows for us:
And the stars may never again shine
as now they shine.
Long before October returns,
Seas of blood will have parted us:
And you must crush the love in your heart,
and I the love in mine!

Emily Brontë

From Dipsychus

(Scene IIA – 'The Quays')

Dipsychus
Could I believe that any child of Eve
Were formed and fashioned, raised and reared for
    nought
But to be swilled with animal delight
And yield five minutes' pleasure to the male –
Could I think cherry lips and stubby cheeks
That seems to exist express for such fond play,
Hold in suppression nought to come; o'ershell

No lurking virtuality of more –

Spirit
It was a lover and his lass,
With a hey and a ho, and a hey nonino!
Betwixt the acres of the rye,
With a hey and a ho, and a hey nonino!
These pretty country folks would lie –
In the spring time, the pretty spring time.

Dipsychus
And could I think I owed it not to her,
In virtue of our manhood's stronger sight,
Even against entreaty to forbear –

Spirit
O Joseph and Don Quixote! This
A chivalry of chasteness is,
That turns to nothing all, that story
Has made out of your ancient glory!
Still I must urge, that though tis sad
Tis sure, once gone, for good or bad
The prize whose loss we are deploring
Is physically past restoring:
C'en est fait. Nor can God's own self
As Coleridge on the dusty shelf
Says in his wicked Omniana
Renew to Ina frail or Ana
The once rent hymenis membrana.
So that it needs consideration
By what more moral occupation
To support this vast population?

Dipsychus
Could I believe that purity were not
Lodged somewhere, precious pearl, e'en underneath
The hardest coarsest outside: could I think
That any heart in woman's bosom set

By tenderness o'ermastering mean desire,
Faithfulness, love, were unredeemable.
Or could I think it sufferable in me
For my poor pleasure's sake to superadd
One possible finger's pressure to the weight
That turns and grinds as in a fierce machine
This hapless kind, these pariahs of the sex –

Spirit
Well; people talk – their sentimentality.
Meantime, as by some sad fatality
Morality is still mortality;
Nor has corruption, spite of facility,
And doctrines of perfectibility
Yet put on incorruptibility,
As women are and the world goes
They're not so badly off – who knows?
They die, as we do in the end;
They marry; or they – *superintend*:
Or Sidney Herberts sometimes rise,
And send them out to colonize.

Dipsychus
Or could I think that it had been for nought
That from my boyhood until now, in spite
Of most misguiding theories, at the moment
Somewhat has ever stepped in to arrest
My ingress at the fatal-closing door,
That many and many a time my foolish foot
O'ertreading the dim sill, spite of itself
And spite of me, instinctively fell back.

Spirit
Like Balaam's ass, in spite of thwacking,
Against the wall his master backing,
Because of something hazy stalking
Just in the way they should be walking –
Soon after too, he took to talking!

Dipsychus

Backed, and refused my bidding – Could I think,
In spite of carnal understanding's sneers,
All this fortuitous only – all a chance?

Spirit

Ah, just what I was going to say;
An Angel met you in the way!
Cry mercy of his heavenly highness –
I took him for that cunning shyness.

Dipsychus

Shyness. Tis but another word for shame;
And that for Sacred Instinct. Off ill thoughts!
Tis holy ground your foot has stepped upon.

Spirit

Ho, Virtue quotha! trust who knows;
There's not a girl that by us goes
But mightn't have you if she chose:
No doubt but you would give her trouble;
But then you'd pay her for it double.
By Jove – if I were but a lass,
I'd soon see what I'd bring to pass.

Dipsychus

O welcome then, the sweet domestic bonds,
The matrimonial sanctities; the hopes
And cares of wedded life; parental thoughts,
The prattle of young children, the good word
Of fellow men, the sanction of the law,
And permanence and habit, that transmute
Grossness itself to crystal. O, why, why,
Why ever let this speculating brain
Rest upon other objects than on this?

Spirit

Well, well – if you must stick perforce

Unto the ancient holy course,
And map your life out on the plan
Of the connubial puritan,
For God's sake carry our your creed,
Go home and marry – and be d – – – – d.
I'll help you.

Dipsychus
You!

Spirit
O never scout me;
I know you'll ne'er propose without me.

Dipsychus
I have talked o'ermuch. The Spirit passes from me.
O folly, folly, what have I done? Ah me!

Spirit
You'd like another turn, I see.
Yes, yes, a little quiet turn.
By all means let us live and learn.
Here's many a lady still waylaying,
And sundry gentlemen purveying.
And if 'twere only just to see
The room of an Italian *fille*,
'Twere worth the trouble and the money.
You'll like to find – I found it funny –
The chamber *où vous faites votre affaire*
Stand nicely fitted up for prayer;
While dim you trace along one end
The Sacred Supper's length extend.
The calm Madonna o'er your head
Smiles, *col bambino*, on the bed
Where – but your chaste ears I must spare –
Where, as we said, *vous faites votre affaire*.
They'll suit you, these Venetian pets!
So natural, not the least coquettes –

Really at times one quite forgets –
Well, would you like perhaps to arrive at
A pretty creature's home in private?
We can look in, just say goodnight,
And, if you like to stay, all right.
Just as you fancy – is it well?

Dipsychus
O folly, folly, folly! To the Hotel!

Arthur Hugh Clough

Douglas, Douglas, Tender and True

Could you come back to me, Douglas, Douglas,
In the old likeness that I knew,
I would be so faithful, so loving, Douglas,
Douglas, Douglas, tender and true.

Never a scornful word should grieve ye,
I'd smile on ye sweet as the angels do;
Sweet as your smile on me shone ever,
Douglas, Douglas, tender and true.

Oh, to call back the days that are not!
My eyes were blinded, your words were few;
Do you know the truth now up in heaven,
Douglas, Douglas, tender and true?

I never was worthy of you, Douglas;
Not half worthy the like of you:
Now all men beside seem to me like shadows –
I love you, Douglas, tender and true.

Stretch out your hand to me, Douglas, Douglas,
Drop forgiveness from heaven like dew;
As I lay my heart on your dead heart, Douglas,
Douglas, Douglas, tender and true.

Dinah Maria Craik

In Memoriam CXXIX

Dear friend, far off, my lost desire,
So far, so near in woe and weal;
O loved the most, when most I feel
There is a lower and a higher;

Known and unknown; human, divine;
Sweet human hand and lips and eye;
Dear heavenly friend that canst not die,
Mine, mine, forever, ever mine;

Strange friend, past, present, and to be;
Loved deeplier, darklier understood;
Behold, I dream a dream of good,
And mingle all the world with thee.

Alfred, Lord Tennyson

The Lark in the Clear Air

Dear thoughts are in my mind
And my soul soars enchanted,
As I hear the sweet lark sing
In the clear air of the day.
For a tender beaming smile
To my hope has been granted,

And tomorrow she shall hear
All my fond heart would say.

I shall tell her all my love,
All my soul's adoration;
And I think she will hear me
And will not say me nay.
It is this that fills my soul
With its joyous elation,
As I hear the sweet lark sing
In the clear air of the day.

Sir Samuel Ferguson

Do You Remember That Night?
(Translation of a 17th century Irish poem)

Do you remember that night
When you were at the window
With neither hat nor gloves
Nor coat to shelter you?
I reached out my hand to you
And you ardently grasped it,
I remained to converse with you
Until the lark began to sing.

Do you remember that night
That you and I were
At the foot of the rowan-tree
And the night drifting snow?
Your head on my breast,
And your pipe sweetly playing?
Little thought I that night
That our love ties would loosen!

Beloved of my inmost heart,
Come some night, and soon,

When my people are at rest,
That we may talk together.
My arms shall encircle you
While I relate my sad tale,
That your soft, pleasant converse
Hath deprived me of heaven.

The fire is unraked,
The light unextinguished,
The key under the door,
Do you softly draw it.
My mother is asleep,
But I am wide awake;
My fortune in my hand,
I am ready to go with you.

Eugene O'Curry

Down By The Salley Gardens

Down by the salley gardens my love and I did meet;
She passed the salley gardens with little snow-white
    feet.
She bid me take love easy, as the leaves grow on the
    tree;
But I, being young and foolish, with her would not
    agree.

In a field by the river my love and I did stand,
And on my leaning shoulder she laid her snow-white
    hand.
She bid me take life easy, as the grass grows on the
    weirs;
But I was young and foolish, and now am full of tears.

W. B. Yeats

Self-Congratulation

Ellen, you were thoughtless once
Of beauty or of grace,
Simple and homely in attire,
Careless of form and face;
Then whence this change? and wherefore now
So often smooth your hair?
And wherefore deck your youthful form
With such unwearied care?

Tell us – and cease to tire our ears
With that familiar strain –
Why will you play those simple tunes
So often, o'er again?
'Indeed, dear friends, I can but say
That childhood's thoughts are gone;
Each year its own new feelings brings,
And years move swiftly on:

'And for these little simple airs –
I love to play them o'er
So much – I dare not promise, now,
To play them never more.'
I answered – and it was enough;
They turned them to depart;
They could not read my secret thoughts,
Nor see my throbbing heart.

I've noticed many a youthful form,
Upon whose changeful face
The inmost workings of the soul
The gazer well might trace;
The speaking eye, the changing lip,
The ready blushing cheek,
The smiling, or beclouded brow,
Their different feelings speak.

But, thank God! you might gaze on mine
For hours, and never know
The secret changes of my soul
From joy to keenest woe.
Last night, as we sat round the fire
Conversing merrily,
We heard, without, approaching steps
Of one well known to me!

There was no trembling in my voice,
No blush upon my cheek,
No lustrous sparkle in my eyes,
Of hope, or joy, to speak;
But, oh! my spirit burned within,
My heart beat full and fast!
He came not nigh – he went away –
And then my joy was past.

And yet my comrades marked it not:
My voice was still the same;
They saw me smile, and o'er my face
No signs of sadness came.
They little knew my hidden thoughts;
And they will *never* know
The aching anguish of my heart,
The bitter burning woe!

Anne Brontë

The Husband Of To-Day

Eyes caught by beauty, fancy by eyes caught;
Sweet possibilities, question, and wonder –
What did her smile say? What has her brain thought?
Her standard, what? Am I o'er it or under?
Flutter in meeting – in absence dreaming;

Tremor in greeting – for meeting scheming;
Caught by the senses, and yet all through
True with the heart of me, sweetheart, to you.

Only the brute in me yields to the pressure
Of longings inherent – of vices acquired;
All this, my darling, is folly – not pleasure,
Only my fancy – not soul – has been fired.
Sense thrills exalted, thrills to love-madness;
Fancy grown sad becomes almost love-sadness;
And yet love has with it nothing to do,
Love is fast fettered, sweetheart, to you.

Lacking fresh fancies, time flags – grows wingless;
Life without folly would fail – fall flat;
But the love that lights life, and makes death's self
    stingless –
You, and you only, have wakened that.
Sweet are all women, you are the best of them;
You are so dear because dear are the rest of them;
After each fancy has sprung, grown, and died,
Back I come ever, dear, to your side.
The strongest of passions – in joy – seeks the new,
But in grief I turn ever, sweetheart, to you.

E. Nesbit

Ballade Of Lovers

Double Refrain

For the man was she made by the Eden tree,
To be decked in soft raiment, and worn on his sleeve,
To be fondled so long as they both agree,
A thing to take, or a thing to leave.

But for her, let her live through one long summer eve,
Just the stars, and the moon, and the man, and she –
And her soul will escape her beyond reprieve,
And, alas! the whole of her world is he.

To-morrow brings plenty as lovesome, maybe –
If she breaks when he handles her, why should he
    grieve?
She is only one pearl in a pearl-crowded sea,
A thing to take, or a thing to leave.
But she, though she knows he has kissed to deceive
And forsakes her, still only clings on at his knee –
When life has gone, what further loss can bereave?
And, alas! the whole of her world is he.

For the man was she made upon Eden lea,
To be helpmeet what time there is burden to heave,
White-footed, to follow where he walks free,
A thing to take, or a thing to leave, –
White-fingered, to weave and to interweave
Her woof with his warp and a tear two or three,
Till clear his way out through her web he cleave,
And, alas! the whole of her world is he.

Envoi

Did he own her no more, when he named her Eve,
Than a thing to take, or a thing to leave?
A flower-filled plot, that unlocks to his key –
But, alas! the whole of her world is he.

May Probyn

Gifts

Give a man a horse he can ride,
Give a man a boat he can sail;
And his rank and wealth, his strength and health,
On sea nor shore shall fail.

Give a man a pipe he can smoke,
Give a man a book he can read:
And his home is bright with a calm delight,
Though the room be poor indeed.

Give a man a girl he can love,
As I, O my love, love thee;
And his heart is great with the pulse of Fate,
At home, on land, on sea.

James Thomson

The Kiss

Give me, my love, that billing kiss
I taught you one delicious night,
When, turning epicures in bliss,
We tried inventions of delight.

Come, gently steal my lips along,
And let your lips in murmurs move, –
Ah, no! – again – that kiss was wrong –
How can you be so dull, my love?

'Cease, cease!' the blushing girl replied –
And in her milky arms she caught me –
'How can you thus your pupil chide;
You know 'twas in the dark you taught me!'

Thomas Moore

Go From Me

(Sonnets from The Portuguese VI)

Go from me. Yet I feel that I shall stand
Henceforward in thy shadow. Nevermore
Alone upon the threshold of my door
Of individual life, I shall command
The uses of my soul, nor lift my hand
Serenely in the sunshine as before,
Without the sense of that which I forbore –
Thy touch upon the palm. The widest land
Doom takes to part us, leaves thy heart in mine
With pulses that beat double. What I do
And what I dream include thee, as the wine
Must taste of its own grapes. And when I sue
God for myself, He hears that name of thine,
And sees within my eyes the tears of two.

Elizabeth Barrett Browning

He Wishes For The Cloths Of Heaven

Had I the heavens' embroidered cloths,
Enwrought with golden and silver light,
The blue and the dim and the dark cloths
Of night and light and the half-light,
I would spread the cloths under your feet:
But I, being poor, have only my dreams;
I have spread my dreams under your feet;
Tread softly because you tread on my dreams.

W. B. Yeats

Song

He climbs his lady's tower where sail
Cold clouds about the moon,
And at his feet the nightingale
Sings – Sir, too soon, too soon!
He steals across his lady's park,
He tries her secret grate,
And overhead the saucy lark
Sings – Sir, too late, too late!

Eleanor Jane Alexander

Envy

He was the first always: Fortune
Shone bright in his face.
I fought for years; with no effort
He conquered the place:
We ran; my feet were all bleeding,
But he won the race.

Spite of his many successes
Men loved him the same;
My one pale ray of good fortune
Met scoffing and blame.
When we erred, they gave him pity,
But me – only shame.

My home was still in the shadow,
His lay in the sun:
I longed in vain: what he asked for
It straightway was done.
Once I staked all my heart's treasure,
We played – and he won.

Yes; and just now I have seen him
Cold, smiling, and blest,
Laid in his coffin. God help me!
While he is at rest,
I am cursed still to live: – even
Death loved him the best.

Adelaide Anne Procter

Corinne's Last Love-Song

How beautiful, how beautiful you streamed upon my
    sight,
In glory and in grandeur, as a gorgeous sunset-light!
How softly, soul-subduing, fell your words upon mine
    ear,
Like low aerial music when some angel hovers near!
What tremulous, faint ecstasy to clasp your hand in
    mine,
Till the darkness fell upon me of a glory too divine!
The air around grew languid with our intermingled
    breath,
And in your beauty's shadow I sank motionless as
    death.
I saw you not, I heard not, for a mist was on my brain –
I only felt that life could give no joy like that again.

And this was Love – I knew it not, but blindly floated
    on,
And now I'm on the ocean waste, dark, desolate, alone;
The waves are raging round me – I'm reckless where
    they guide;
No hope is left to light me, no strength to stem the tide.
As a leaf along the torrent, a cloud across the sky,
As dust upon the whirlwind, so my life is drifting by.
The dream that drank the meteor's light – the form from

Heav'n has flown –
The vision and the glory, they are passing – they are
    gone.
Oh! love is frantic agony, and life one throb of pain;
Yet I would bear its darkest woes to dream that dream
    again.

Jane, Lady Wilde ('Speranza')

How Do I Love Thee?
(Sonnet from the Portuguese XLII)

How do I love thee? Let me count the ways.
I love thee to the depth, and breadth, and height
My soul can reach, when feeling out of sight
For the ends of being and ideal grace.
I love thee to the level of every day's
Most quiet need, by sun and candlelight.
I love thee freely, as men strive for right:
I love thee purely, as they turn from praise.
I love thee with the passion put to use
In my old griefs, and with my childhood's faith.
I love thee with a love I seemed to lose
With my lost saints. I love thee with the breath,
Smiles, tears, of all my life – and if God choose,
I shall but love thee better after death.

Elizabeth Barrett Browning

Song

How many times do I love thee, dear?
Tell me how many thoughts there be
In the atmosphere

Of a new fallen year,
Whose white and sable hours appear
The latest flake of Eternity:
So many times do I love thee, dear.

How many times do I love again?
Tell me how many beads there are
In a silver chain
Of evening rain,
Unravelled from the tumbling main,
And threading the eye of a yellow star:
So many times do I love again.

Thomas Lovell Beddoes

From Amours De Voyage

Claude To Eustace

I am in love, meantime, you think; no doubt you would
    think so.
I am in love, you say; with those letters, of course, you
    would say so.
I am in love, you declare. I think not so; yet I grant you
It is a pleasure indeed to converse with this girl. Oh,
    rare gift,
Rare felicity, this! she can talk in a rational way, can
Speak upon subjects that really are matters of mind and
    of thinking,
Yet in perfection retain her simplicity; never, one
    moment,
Never, however you urge it, however you tempt her,
    consents to
Step from ideas and fancies and loving sensations to
    those vain
Conscious understandings that vex the minds of man-
    kind.

No, though she talk, it is music; her fingers desert not
the keys; 'tis
Song, though you hear in the song the articulate
vocables sounded,
Syllabled singly and sweetly the words of melodious
meaning.
I am in love, you say; I do not think so, exactly.

Claude to Eustace

There are two different kinds, I believe, of human
attraction:
One which simply disturbs, unsettles, and makes you
uneasy.
And another that poises, retains, and fixes and holds
you.
I have no doubt, for myself, in giving my voice for the
latter.
I do not wish to be moved, but growing where I was
growing,
There more truly to grow, to live where as yet I had
languished
I do not like being moved: for the will is excited; and
action
Is a most dangerous thing; I tremble for something
factitious,
Some malpractice of heart: and illegitimate process;
We are so prone to these things with our terrible
notions of duty.

Arthur Hugh Clough

To My Wife
With A Copy Of My Poem

I can write no stately poem
As a prelude to my lay;
From a poet to a poem
I would dare to say.

For if of these fallen petals
One to you seem fair,
Love will waft it till it settles
On your hair.

And when wind and winter harden
All the loveless land,
It will whisper of the garden,
You will understand.

Oscar Wilde

The Lust Of The Eyes

I care not for my Lady's soul
Though I worship before her smile;
I care not where be my Lady's goal
When her beauty shall lose its wile.

Low sit I down at my Lady's feet
Gazing through her wild eyes
Smiling to think how my love will fleet
When their starlike beauty dies.

I care not if my Lady pray
To our Father which is in Heaven
But for joy my heart's quick pulses play
For to me her love is given.

Then who shall close my Lady's eyes
And who shall fold her hands?
Will any hearkèn if she cries
Up to the unknown lands?

Elizabeth Siddal

Trinity

I did not love him for myself alone:
I loved him that he loved my dearest love.
O God, no blasphemy
It is to feel we loved in trinity,
To tell Thee that I loved him as Thy Dove
Is loved, and is Thy own,
That comforted the moan
Of Thy Beloved, when earth could give no balm
And in Thy Presence makes His tenderest calm.

So I possess this creature of Love's flame,
So loving what I love he lives from me;
Not white, a thing of fire,
Of seraph plumèd limbs and one desire,
That is my heart's own, and shall ever be:
An animal – with aim
Thy Dove avers the same . . .
O symbol of our perfect union, strange
Unconscious Bearer of Love's interchange.

Michael Field

From The Ring And The Book

I do but play with an imagined life
Of who, unfettered by a vow, unblessed
By the higher call, – since you will have it so, –
Leads it companioned by the woman there,
To live, and see her learn, and learn by her,
Out of the low obscure and petty world –
Or only see one purpose and one will
Evolve themselves i' the world, change wrong to right:
To have to do with nothing but the true,
The good, the eternal – and these, not alone
In the main current of the general life,
But small experiences of every day,
Concerns of the particular hearth and home:
To learn not only by a comet's rush
But a rose's birth, – not by the grandeur, God –
But the comfort, Christ. All this, how far away!
Mere delectation, meet for a minute's dream! –
Just as a drudging student trims his lamp,
Opens his Plutarch, puts him in the place
Of Roman, Grecian; draws the patched gown close,
Dreams, 'Thus should I fight, save or rule the world!'
Then smilingly, contentedly, awakes
To the old solitary nothingness,
So I, from such communion, pass content . . .

O great, just, good God! Miserable me!

Robert Browning

The Wife Of All Ages

I do not catch these subtle shades of feeling,
Your fine distinctions are too fine for me;
This meeting, scheming, longing, trembling, dreaming,

To me mean love, and only love, you see;
In me at least 'tis love, you will admit,
And you the only man who wakens it.

Suppose *I* yearned, and longed, and dreamed, and
   fluttered,
What would you say or think, or further, do?
Why should one rule be fit for me to follow,
While there exists a different law for you?
If all these fires and fancies came my way,
Would you believe love was so far away?

On all these other women – never doubt it –
'Tis love you lavish, love you promised me!
What do I care to be the first, or fiftieth?
It is the *only one* I care to be.
Dear, I would be your sun, as mine you are,
Not the most radiant wonder of a star.

And so, good-bye! Among such sheaves of roses
You will not miss the flower I take from you;
Amid the music of so many voices
You will forget the little songs I knew –
The foolish tender words I used to say,
The little common sweets of every day.

The world, no doubt, has fairest fruits and blossoms
To give to you; but what, ah! what for me?
Nay, after all I am your slave and bondmaid,
And all my world is in my slavery.
So, as before, I welcome any part
Which you may choose to give me of your heart.

E. Nesbit

Love's Story

I do not love thee,
So I'll not deceive thee,
I do not love thee,
Yet I'm loth to leave thee.

I do not love thee,
Yet joy's very essence
Comes with thy footstep,
Is complete in thy presence.

I do not love thee,
Yet when gone I sigh
And think about thee
'Till the stars all die.

I do not love thee,
Yet thy black bright eyes
Bring to my heart's soul
Heaven and paradise.

I do not love thee,
Yet thy handsome ways
Bring me in absence
Almost hopeless days.

I cannot hate thee,
Yet my love seems debtor
To love thee more
So hating, love thee better.

John Clare

I Do Not Love Thee

I do not love thee! No! I do not love thee!
And yet when thou art absent I am sad;
And envy even the bright blue sky above thee,
Whose quiet stars may see thee and be glad.

I do not love thee! yet, I know not why,
Whate'er thou does seems still well done, to me –
And often in my solitude I sigh –
That those I do love are not more like thee!

I do not love thee! yet when thou art gone
I hate the sound (though those who speak be dear)
Which breaks the lingering echo of the tone
Thy voice of music leaves upon my ear.

I do not love thee! yet thy speaking eyes,
With their deep, bright and most expressive blue –
Between me and the midnight heaven arise,
Oftener than any eyes I ever knew.

I know I do not love thee! yet, alas!
Others will scarcely trust my candid heart;
And oft I catch them smiling as they pass,
Because they see me gazing where thou art.

Caroline Norton

Natural Selection

I had found out a gift for my fair,
I had found where the cave-men were laid;
Skull, femur, and pelvis were there,
And spears, that of silex they made.

But he ne'er could be true, she averred,
Who would dig up an ancestor's grave –
And I loved her the more when I heard
Such filial regard for the Cave.

My shelves, they are furnished with stones
All sorted and labelled with care,
And a splendid collection of bones,
Each one of them ancient and rare;

One would think she might like to retire
To my study – she calls it a 'hole!'
Not a fossil I heard her admire,
But I begged it, or borrowed, or stole.

But there comes an idealess lad,
With a strut, and a stare, and a smirk;
And I watch, scientific though sad,
The Law of Selection at work.

Of Science he hasn't a trace,
He seeks not the How and the Why,
But he sings with an amateur's grace,
And he dances much better than I.

And we know the more dandified males
By dance and by song win their wives –
'Tis a law that with *Aves* prevails,
And even in *Homo* survives.

Shall I rage as they whirl in the valse?
Shall I sneer as they carol and coo?
Ah no! for since Chloe is false,
I'm certain that Darwin is true!

Constance Naden

Sudden Light

I have been here before,
But when or how I cannot tell:
I know the grass beyond the door,
The sweet keen smell,
The sighing sound, the lights around the shore.

You have been mine before –
How long ago I may not know:
But just when at that swallow's soar
Your neck turned so,
Some veil did fall, – I knew it all of yore.

Then, now, – perchance again! . . .
O round mine eyes your tresses shake!
Shall we not lie as we have lain
Thus for Love's sake,
And sleep, and wake, yet never break the chain?

Dante Gabriel Rossetti

Terenure

I laughed at the lovers I passed
Two and two in the shadows,
I, solitary as one old horse I saw
Alone in the meadows.
The lovers so many I passed,
In mute embraces:
A roadside flower, joy,
In the hid places.
I wondered, sure, to notice joy
As common as a weed –
Out of my loneliness wondering,
Laughing, indeed.

I loved all the lovers I passed
Two and two in the shadows:
I solitary as one old horse, was standing
Alone in the meadows

Blanaid Salkeld

My Lady

I loved her for that she was beautiful;
And that to me she seemed to be all Nature,
And all varieties of things in one:
Would set at night in clouds of tears, and rise
All light and laughter in the morning, fear
No petty customs nor appearances;
But think what others only dreamed about;
And say what others did but think, and do
What others dared but do: so pure withal
In soul; in heart and act such conscious yet
Such perfect innocence, she made round her
A halo of delight. 'Twas these which won me;
And that she never schooled within her breast
One thought or feeling, but gave holiday
To all; and that she made all even mine
In the communion of love: and we
Grew like each other, for we loved each other;
She, mild and generous as the air in spring;
And I, like earth all budding out with love.

Philip James Bailey

Song

I made another garden, yea,
For my new Love:
I left the dead rose where it lay
And set the new above.
Why did my Summer not begin?
Why did my heart not haste?
My old Love came and walked therein,
And laid the garden waste.

She entered with her weary smile,
Just as of old;
She looked around a little while
And shivered with the cold:
Her passing touch was death to all,
Her passing look a blight;
She made the white rose-petals fall,
And turned the red rose white.

Her pale robe clinging to the grass
Seemed like a snake
That bit the grass and ground, alas!
And a sad trail did make.
She went up slowly to the gate,
And then, just as of yore,
She turned back at the last to wait
And say farewell once more.

Arthur William Edgar O'Shaughnessy

Renouncement

I must not think of thee; and, tired yet strong,
I shun the thought that lurks in all delight –
The thought of thee – and in the blue heaven's height,

And in the sweetest passage of a song.
O just beyond the fairest thoughts that throng
This breast, the thought of thee waits, hidden yet bright;
But it must never, never come in sight;
I must stop short of thee the whole day long.
But when sleep comes to close each difficult day,
When night gives pause to the long watch I keep,
And all my bonds I needs must loose apart,
And doff my will as raiment laid away, –
With the first dream that comes with the first sleep,
I run, I run, I am gathered to thy heart.

Alice Meynell

Love In Mayfair

I must tell you, my dear,
I'm in love with him vastly!
Twenty thousand a year,
I must tell you, my dear!
He will soon be a peer –
And such diamonds! – and, lastly,
I must tell you, my dear,
I'm in love with him, vastly!

May Probyn

First Love

I ne'er was struck before that hour
With love so sudden and so sweet,
Her face it bloomed like a sweet flower
And stole my heart away complete.
My face turned pale as deadly pale,

My legs refused to walk away,
And when she looked, what could I ail?
My life and all seemed turned to clay.

And then my blood rushed to my face
And took my eyesight quite away,
The trees and bushes round the place
Seemed midnight at noonday.
I could not see a single thing,
Words from my eyes did start –
They spoke as chords do from the string,
And blood burnt round my heart.

Are flowers the winter's choice?
Is love's bed always snow?
She seemed to hear my silent voice,
Not love's appeals to know.
I never saw so sweet a face
As that I stood before.
My heart has left its dwelling-place
And can return no more.

John Clare

The Last Ride Together

I said – Then, dearest, since 'tis so,
Since now at length my fate I know,
Since nothing all my love avails,
Since all, my life seemed meant for, fails,
Since this was written and needs must be –
My whole heart rises up to bless
Your name in pride and thankfulness!
Take back the hope you gave, – I claim
Only a memory of the same,

– And this beside, if you will not blame,
Your leave for one more last ride with me.

My mistress bent that brow of hers;
Those deep dark eyes where pride demurs
When pity would be softening through,
Fixed me a breathing while or two
With life or death in the balance: right!
The blood replenished me again;
My last thought was at least not vain:
I and my mistress, side by side,
Shall be together, breathe and ride,
So, one day more am I deified.
Who knows but the world may end tonight?

Hush! if you saw some western cloud
All billowy-bosomed, over-bowed
By many benedictions – sun's
And moon's and evening-star's at once –
And so, you, looking and loving best,
Conscious grew, your passion drew
Cloud, sunset, moonrise, star-shine too,
Down on you, near and yet more near,
Till flesh must fade for heaven was here! –
Thus leant she and lingered – joy and fear!
Thus lay she a moment on my breast.

Then we began to ride. My soul
Smoothed itself out, a long-cramped scroll
Freshening and fluttering in the wind.
Past hopes already lay behind.
What need to strive with a life awry?
Had I said that, had I done this,
So might I gain, so might I miss.
Might she have loved me? just as well
She might have hated, who can tell!
Where had I been now if the worst befell?
And here we are riding, she and I.

Fall I alone, in words and deeds?
Why, all men strive and who succeeds?
We rode; it seemed my spirit flew,
Saw other regions, cities new,
As the world rushed by on either side.
I thought, – All labour, yet no less
Bear up beneath their unsuccess.
Look at the end of work, contrast
The petty done, the undone vast,
This present of theirs with the hopeful past!
I hoped she would love me; here we ride.

What hand and brain went ever paired?
What heart alike conceived and dared?
What act proved all its thought had been?
What will but felt the fleshly screen?
We ride and I see her bosom heave.
There's many a crown for who can reach.
Ten lines, a statesman's life in each!
The flag stuck on a heap of bones,
A soldier's doing! what atones?
They scratch his name on the Abbey-stones.
My riding is better, by their leave.

What does it all mean, poet? Well,
Your brains beat into rhythm, you tell
What we felt only; you expressed
You hold things beautiful the best,
And pace them in rhyme so, side by side.
'Tis something, nay 'tis much: but then,
Have you yourself what's best for men?
Are you – poor, sick, old ere your time –
Nearer one whit your own sublime
Than we who never have turned a rhyme?
Sing, riding's a joy! For me, I ride.

And you, great sculptor – so, you gave
A score of years to Art, her slave,

And that's your Venus, whence we turn
To yonder girl that fords the burn!
You acquiesce, and shall I repine?
What, man of music, you grown grey
With notes and nothing else to say,
Is this your sole praise from a friend,
'Greatly his opera's strains intend,
Put in music we know how fashions end!'
I gave my youth; but we ride, in fine.

Who knows what's fit for us? Had fate
Proposed bliss here should sublimate
My being – had I signed the bond –
Still one must lead some life beyond,
Have a bliss to die with, dim-descried.
This foot once planted on the goal,
This glory-garland round my soul,
Could I descry such? Try and test!
I sink back shuddering from the quest.
Earth being so good, would heaven seem best?
Now, heaven and she are beyond this ride.

And yet – she has not spoke so long!
What if heaven be that, fair and strong
At life's best, with our eyes upturned
Whither life's flower is first discerned,
We, fixed so, ever should so abide?
What if we still ride on, we two
With life for ever old yet new,
Changed not in kind but in degree,
The instant made eternity, –
And heaven just prove that I and she
Ride, ride together, for ever ride?

Robert Browning

And Then No More

I saw her once, one little while, and then no more:
'Twas Eden's light on Earth awhile, and then no more:
Amid the throng she passed along the meadow-floor:
Spring seemed to smile on Earth awhile, and then no
    more:
But whence she came, which way she went, what garb
    she wore
I noted not; I gazed awhile, and then no more!

I saw her once, one little while, and then no more:
'Twas Paradise on Earth awhile, and then no more.
Ah! what avail my vigils pale, my magic lore?
She shone before mine eyes awhile, and then no more.
The shallop of my peace is wrecked on Beauty's shore.
Near Hope's fair isle it rode awhile, and then no more!

I saw her once, one little while, and then no more:
Earth looked like Heaven a little while, and then no
    more.
Her presence thrilled and lighted to its inner core
My desert breast a little while, and then no more.
So may, perchance, a meteor glance at midnight o'er
Some ruined pile a little while, and then no more!

I saw her once, one little while, and then no more:
The earth was Peri-land awhile, and then no more.
Oh, might I see but once again, as once before,
Through chance or wile, that shape awhile, and
    then no more!
Death soon would heal my griefs! This heart, now sad
    and sore,
Would beat anew a little while, and then no more.

James Clarence Mangan

The Kiss

'I saw you take his kiss!' ''Tis true.'
'O, modesty!' ''Twas strictly kept:'

He thought me asleep; at least, I knew
He thought I thought he thought I slept.'

Coventry Patmore

Any Husband To Many A Wife

I scarcely know my worthless picture,
As seen in those soft eyes and clear;
But oh, dear heart, I fear the stricture
You pass on it when none are near.

Deep eyes that smiling give denial
To tears that you have shed in vain;
Fond heart that summoned on my trial,
Upbraids the witness of its pain.

Eyes, tender eyes, betray me never!
Still hold the flattered image fast
Whereby I shape the fond endeavour
To justify your faith at last.

Emily Pfeiffer

Farewell To Juliet

I see you, Juliet, still, with your straw hat
Loaded with vines, and with your dear pale face,
On which those thirty years so lightly sat,

And the white outline of your muslin dress.
You wore a little fichu trimmed with lace
And crossed in front, as was the fashion then,
Bound at your waist with a broad band or sash,
All white and fresh and virginally plain.
There was a sound of shouting far away
Down in the valley, as they called to us,
And you, with hands clasped seeming still to pray
Patience of fate, stood listening to me thus
With heaving bosom. There a rose lay curled.
It was the reddest rose in all the world.

Wilfrid Scawen Blunt

To Mary

I sleep with thee, and wake with thee,
And yet thou art not there;
I fill my arms with thoughts of thee,
And press the common air.
Thy eyes are gazing upon mine,
When thou art out of sight;
My lips are always touching thine,
At morning, noon, and night.

I think and speak of other things
To keep my mind at rest:
But still to thee my memory clings
Like love in woman's breast.
I hide it from the world's wide eye,
And think and speak contrary;
But soft the wind comes from the sky,
And whispers tales of Mary.

The night wind whispers in my ear,
The moon shines in my face;

A burden still of chilling fear
I find in every place.
The breeze is whispering in the bush
And the dews fall from the tree,
All sighing on, and will not hush,
Some pleasant tales of thee.

John Clare

Second Thoughts

I thought of leaving her for a day
In town, it was such iron winter
At Durdans, the garden frosty clay,
The woods as dry as any splinter,
The sky congested. I would break
From the deep, lethargic, country air
To the shining lamps, to the clash of the play,
And to-morrow, wake
Beside her, a thousand things to say.
I planned – O more – I had almost started; –
I lifted her face in my hands to kiss, –
A face in a border of fox's fur,
For the bitter black wind had stricken her,
And she wore it – her soft hair straying out
Where it buttoned against the gray, leather snout:
In an instant we should have parted;
But at sight of the delicate world within
That fox-fur collar, from brow to chin,
At sight of those wonderful eyes from the mine,
Coal pupils, an iris of glittering spa,
And the wild, ironic, defiant shine
As of a creature behind a bar
One has captured, and, when three lives are past,
May hope to reach the heart of at last,
All that, and the love at her lips combined

To shew me what folly it were to miss
A face with such thousand things to say,
And beside these, such thousand more to spare,
For the shining lamps, for the clash of the play –
O madness, not for a single day
Could I leave her! I stayed behind.

Michael Field

The Arrow

I thought of your beauty, and this arrow,
Made out of a wild thought, is in my marrow.
There's no man may look upon her, no man,
As when newly grown to be a woman,
Tall and noble but with face and bosom
Delicate in colour as apple blossom.
This beauty's kinder, yet for a reason
I could weep that the old is out of season.

W. B. Yeats

Mary's Song

I wad hae gi'en him my lips tae kiss,
Had I been his, had I been his –
Barley breid and elder wine,
Had I been his, as he is mine.

The wanderin' bee it seeks the rose,
Tae the lochan's bosom the burnie goes.
A wild bird cries at evenin's fa',
'Rise up my love an' come awa'.'

My Beloved sail hae this hert tae braik,
The reid reid wine and the barley cake.
A hert tae braik and a mou' tae kiss,
Tho' he be nae mine as I am his.

Marion Angus

The Song of Wandering Aengus

I went out to the hazel wood,
Because a fire was in my head,
And cut and peeled a hazel wand,
And hooked a berry to a thread;
And when white moths were on the wing,
And moth-like stars were flickering out,
I dropped the berry in a stream
And caught a little silver trout.

When I had laid it on the floor
I went to blow the fire aflame,
But something rustled on the floor,
And some one called me by my name:
It had become a glimmering girl
With apple blossom in her hair
Who called me by my name and ran
And faded through the brightening air.

Though I am old with wandering
Through hollow lands and hilly lands,
I will find out where she has gone,
And kiss her lips and take her hands;
And walk among long dappled grass,
And pluck till time and times are done
The silver apples of the moon,
The golden apples of the sun.

W. B. Yeats

Ringsend

(After reading Tolstoi)

I will live in Ringsend
With a red-headed whore,
And the fan-light gone in
Where it lights the hall-door;
And listen each night
For her querulous shout,
As at last she streels in
And the pubs empty out.
To soothe that wild breast
With my old-fangled songs,
Till she feels it redressed
From inordinate wrongs,
Imagined, outrageous,
Preposterous wrongs,
Till peace at last comes,
Shall be all I will do,
Where the little lamp blooms
Like a rose in the stew;
And up the back-garden
The sound comes to me
Of the lapsing, unsoilable,
Whispering sea.

Oliver St John Gogarty

Romance

I will make you brooches and toys for your delight
Of bird-song at morning and star-shine at night.
I will make a palace fit for you and me,
Of green days in forests and blue days at sea.

I will make my kitchen, and you shall keep your room,
Where white flows the river and bright blows the
    broom,
And you shall wash your linen and keep your body
    white
In rainfall at morning and dewfall at night.

And this shall be for music when no one else is near,
The fine song for singing, the rare song to hear!
That only I remember, that only you admire,
Of the broad road that stretches and the roadside fire.

Robert Louis Stevenson

The First Day

I wish I could remember the first day,
First hour, first moment of your meeting me,
If bright or dim the season, it might be
Summer or Winter for aught that I can say;
So unrecorded did it slip away,
So blind was I to see and to foresee,
So dull to mark the budding of my tree
That would not blossom yet for many a May.
If only I could recollect it, such
A day of days! I let it come and go
As traceless as a thaw of bygone snow;
It seemed to mean so little, meant so much;
If only now I could recall that touch,
First touch of hand in hand – Did one but know!

Christina Rossetti

If Grief For Grief Can Touch Thee

If grief for grief can touch thee,
If answering woe for woe,
If any ruth can melt thee,
Come to me now!

I cannot be more lonely,
More drear I cannot be!
My worn heart throbs so wildly
'Twill break for thee.

And when the world despises,
When heaven repels my prayer,
Will not mine angel comfort?
Mine idol hear?

Yes, by the tears I've poured,
By all my hours of pain,
O I shall surely win thee,
Beloved, again!

Emily Brontë

The Penalty of Love

If love should count you worthy, and should deign
One day to seek your door and be your guest,
Pause! ere you draw the bolt and bid him rest,
If in your old content you would remain.
For not alone he enters: in his train
Are angels of the mists, the lonely quest,
Dreams of the unfulfilled and unpossessed,
And sorrow, and life's immemorial pain.
He wakes desires you never may forget,
He shows you stars you never saw before,

He makes you share with him for evermore,
The burden of the world's divine regret.
How wise were you to open not! – and yet,
How poor if you should turn him from the door.

Sidney Royse Lysaght

If The Past Year Were Offered Me Again
(From A Woman's Sonnets I)

If the past year were offered me again,
And choice of good and ill before me set
Would I accept the pleasure with the pain
Or dare to wish that we had never met?
Ah! could I bear those happy hours to miss
When love began, unthought of and unspoke –
That summer day when by a sudden kiss
We knew each other's secret and awoke?
Ah no! not even to escape the pain,
Debate and anguish that I underwent
Flying from thee and my own self in vain
With trouble wasted, till my strength all spent
I knew at last that thou or love or fate
Had conquered and repentance was too late.

Augusta, Lady Gregory

If Thou Must Love Me
(Sonnets from The Portuguese XIV)

If thou must love me, let it be for nought
Except for love's sake only. Do not say
'I love her for her smile . . . her look . . . her way

Of speaking gently . . . for a trick of thought
That falls in well with mine, and certes brought
A sense of pleasant ease on such a day' –
For these things in themselves, Belovèd, may
Be changed, or change for thee, – and love, so wrought,
May be unwrought so. Neither love me for
Thine own dear pity's wiping my cheeks dry, –
A creature might forget to weep, who bore
Thy comfort long, and lose thy love thereby!
But love me for love's sake, that evermore
Thou mayst love on, through love's eternity.

Elizabeth Barrett Browning

A Valediction

If we must part,
Then let it be like this;
Not heart on heart,
Nor with the useless anguish of a kiss;
But touch mine hand and say:
'Until to-morrow or some other day,
If we must part.'

Words are so weak
When love hath been so strong:
Let silence speak:
'Life is a little while, and love is long;
A time to sow and reap,
And after harvest a long time to sleep,
But words are weak.'

Ernest Dowson

If

If you and I were but estranged
We might make up another day;
Our hearts still patient and unchanged
Would surely find the way:
But seeing you are dead, my dear,
There's no more to be said.

If I had loved you long in vain
Or your dear love had taken wings,
My Love, that went might come again,
And life is long for righting things:
But seeing you are dead, my dear,
There's no more to be said.

If I might see you in the street
To-day, or any day to come,
Sometimes on faces that I meet
A look of you will strike me dumb:
But seeing you are dead, my dear,
There's no more to be said.

If we but breathed the self-same air
And saw the self-same moon and sun,
If you were living anywhere!
The grass grows by your tall headstone:
And seeing you are dead, my dear,
There's no more to be said.

Katharine Tynan

Lament Of The Irish Emigrant

I'm sittin' on the stile, Mary,
Where we sat side by side
On a bright May mornin' long ago,
When first you were my bride;
The corn was springin' fresh and green,
And the lark sang loud and high –
And the red was on your lip, Mary,
And the love-light in your eye.

The place is little changed, Mary,
The day is bright as then,
The lark's loud song is in my ear,
And the corn is green again;
But I miss the soft clasp of your hand,
And your breath warm on my cheek,
And I still keep list'ning for the words
You never more will speak.

'Tis but a step down yonder lane,
And the little church stands near,
The church where we were wed, Mary,
I see the spire from here.
But the graveyard lies between, Mary,
And my step might break your rest –
For I've laid you, darling! down to sleep,
With your baby on your breast.

I'm very lonely now, Mary,
For the poor make no new friends,
But, O, they love the better still,
The few our Father sends!
And you were all *I* had, Mary,
My blessin' and my pride:
There's nothin' left to care for now,
Since my poor Mary died.

Yours was the good, brave heart, Mary,
That still kept hoping on,
When the trust in God had left my soul,
And my arm's young strength was gone:
There was comfort ever on your lip,
And the kind look on your brow –
I bless you, Mary, for that same,
Though you cannot hear me now.

I thank you for the patient smile
When your heart was fit to break,
When the hunger pain was gnawin' there,
And you hid it, for my sake!
I bless you for the pleasant word,
When your heart was sad and sore –
O, I'm thankful you are gone, Mary,
Where grief can't reach you more!

I'm biddin' you a long farewell,
My Mary – kind and true!
But I'll not forget you, darling!
In the land I'm going to;
They say there's bread and work for all,
And the sun shines always there –
But I'll not forget old Ireland,
Were it fifty times as fair!

And often in those grand old woods
I'll sit, and shut my eyes,
And my heart will travel back again
To the place where Mary lies;
And I'll think I see the little stile
Where we sat side by side:
And the springin' corn, and the bright May morn,
When first you were my bride.

Helen Selina, Lady Dufferin

Kate Dalrymple

In a wee cot-house far across the muir,
Where the peesweeps, plovers, and whaups cry dreary,
There lived an auld maid for mony lang years,
Wham ne'er a wooer did e'er ca' his dearie.
A lanely lass was Kate Dalrymple,
A thrifty quean was Kate Dalrymple;
Nae music, exceptin' the clear burnie's wimple,
Was heard round the dwellin' o' Kate Dalrymple.

Her face had a smack o' the gruesome and grim,
While did frae the fash o' a'wooers defend her;
Her lang Roman nose nearly met wi' her chin,
That brang folk in min' o' the auld witch o' Endor.
A weegle in her walk had Kate Dalrymple,
A sneevil in her talk had Kate Dalrymple;
And mony a cornelian and cairngorm pimple
Did bleeze on the dun face o' Kate Dalrymple.

She span tarry woo' the hale winter through,
For Kate ne'er was lazy, but eident and thrifty;
She wrocht 'mang the peats, coiled the hay, shore the
    corn,
And supported hersel' by her ain shift aye.
But ne'er a lover cam' to Kate Dalrymple,
For beauty and tocher wanted Kate Dalrymple;
Unheeded was she by baith gentle and simple,
A blank in the warld seem'd puir Kate Dalrymple.

But mony are the ups and the downs in life, –
Aft the dice-box o' fate's jumbled a' tapsalteerie;
Sae Kate fell heiress to a friend's hale estate,
And nae langer for lovers had she cause to weary.
The Squire cam' a-wooing soon o' Kate Dalrymple,
The Priest, scrapin', booin', fan' out Kate Dalrymple;
And on ilk wooer's face was seen love's smiling dimple,
And now she's nae mair Kate – but *Miss Dalrymple*.

Her auld currystool, that she used at her wheel,
Is flung by for the saft gilded sofa sae gaudy;
And now she's arrayed in her silks and brocade,
And can rank now for ruffs and muffs wi' ony lady.
Still an unco fash to Kate Dalrymple,
Was dressing and party clash to Kate Dalrymple;
She thocht a half-marow, bred in line mair simple,
Wad be a far fitter match for Kate Dalrymple.

She aftentimes thocht, when she dwelt by hersel',
She could wed Willie Speedyspool, the sarkin' weaver;
And now to the wabster she the secret did tell,
And for love or for int'rest, Will did kindly receive her.
He flang by his heddles soon for Kate Dalrymple,
He brunt a' his treddles doun for Kate Dalrymple;
Though his right e'e doth skellie, and his lang leg doth
    limp ill,
He's wedded to and bedded noo wi' Kate Dalrymple.

William Watt

The Sweet Hussy

In his early days he was quite surprised
When she told him she was compromised
By meetings and lingerings at his whim,
And thinking not of herself but him;
While she lifted orbs aggrieved and round
That scandal should so soon abound,
(As she had raised them to nine or ten
Of antecedent nice young men):
And in remorse he thought with a sigh,
How good she is, and how bad am I! –
It was years before he understood
That she was the wicked one – he the good.

Thomas Hardy

In Love, If Love Be Love
(From Merlin and Vivien)

In love, if love be Love, if love be ours,
Faith and unfaith can ne'er be equal powers:
Unfaith in aught is want of faith in all.

It is the little rift within the lute,
That by and by will make the music mute,
And ever widening slowly silence all.

The little rift within the lover's lute
Or little pitted speck in garnered fruit,
That rotting inward slowly molders all.

It is not worth the keeping: let it go:
But shall it? answer, darling, answer, no.
And trust me not at all or all in all.

Alfred, Lord Tennyson

In Summer's Mellow Midnight

In summer's mellow midnight
A cloudless moon shone through
Our open parlour window
And rosetrees wet with dew –

I sat in silent musing –
The soft wind waved my hair
It told me Heaven was glorious
And sleeping Earth was fair

I needed not its breathing
To bring such thoughts to me
But still it whispered lowly
'How dark the woods will be! –

'The thick leaves in my murmur
Are rustling like a dream,
And all their myriad voices
Instinct with spirit seem.'

I said, 'Go gentle singer,
Thy wooing voice is kind
But do not think to music
Has power to reach my mind –

'Play with the scented flower,
The young tree's supple bough –
And leave my human feelings
In their own course to flow'

The Wanderer would not leave me
Its kiss grew warmer still –
'O come,' it sighed so sweetly
'I'll win thee 'gainst thy will –

'Have we not been from childhood friends?
Have I not loved thee long?
As long as thou hast loved the night
Whose silence wakes my song?

'And when thy heart is laid at rest
Beneath the church-yard stone
I shall have time enough to mourn
And thou to be alone' –

Emily Brontë

The Cold Change

In the cold change which time hath wrought on love
(The snowy winter of his summer prime),
Should a chance sigh or sudden tear-drop move
Thy heart to memory of the olden time;
Turn not to gaze on with pitying eyes,
Nor mock me with a withered hope renewed;
But from the bower we both have loved, arise
And leave me to my barren solitude!

What boots it that a momentary flame
Shoots from the ashes of a dying fire?
We gaze upon the hearth from whence it came,
And know the exhausted embers must expire:
Therefore no pity, or my heart will break;
Be cold, be careless – for thy past love's sake!

Caroline Norton

An Interlude

In the greenest growth of the Maytime,
I rode where the woods were wet,
Between the dawn and the daytime;
The spring was glad that we met.

There was something the season wanted,
Though the ways and the woods smelt sweet;
The breath at your lips that panted,
The pulse of the grass at your feet.

You came, and the sun came after,
And the green grew golden above;
And the flag flowers lightened with laughter,
And the meadowsweet shook with love.

Your feet in the full-grown grasses
Moved soft as a weak wind blows;
You passed me as April passes,
With face made out of a rose.

By the stream where the stems were slender,
Your bright foot paused at the sedge;
It might be to watch the tender
Light leaves in the springtime hedge,

On boughs that the sweet month blanches
With flowery frost of May:
It might be a bird in the branches,
It might be a thorn in the way.

I waited to watch you linger
With foot drawn back from the dew,
Till a sunbeam straight like a finger
Stuck sharp through the leaves at you.

And a bird overheard sang *Follow,*
And a bird to the right sang *Here;*
And the arch of the leaves was hollow,
And the meaning of May was clear.

I saw where the sun's hand pointed,
I knew what the bird's note said;
By the dawn and the dewfall anointed,
You were queen by the gold on your head.

As the glimpse of a burnt-out ember
Recalls a regret of the sun,
I remember, forget, and remember
What Love saw done and undone.

I remember the way we parted,
The day and the way we met;
You hoped we were both brokenhearted,
And knew we should both forget.

And May with her world in flower
Seemed still to murmur and smile
As you murmured and smiled for an hour;
I saw you turn at the stile.

A hand like a white wood-blossom
You lifted, and waved, and passed
With head hung down to the bosom,
And pale, as it seemed, at last.

And the best and the worst of this is
That neither is most to blame
If you've forgotten my kisses
And I've forgotten your name.

Algernon Charles Swinburne

In The Spring
(From Locksley Hall)

In the Spring a fuller crimson comes upon the robin's
   breast;
In the Spring the wanton lapwing gets himself another
   crest;

In the Spring a livelier iris changes on the burnished
   dove;
In the Spring a young man's fancy lightly turns to
   thoughts of love.

Then her cheek was pale and thinner than should be for
    one so young,
And her eyes on all my motions with a mute observance
    hung.

And I said, 'My cousin Amy, speak, and speak the truth
    to me,
Trust me, cousin, all the current of my being sets to
    thee.'

On her pallid cheek and forehead came a colour and a
    light,
As I have seen the rosy red flushing in the northern
    night.

And she turned – her bosom shaken with a sudden
    storm of sighs –
All the spirit deeply dawning in the dark of hazel eyes –

Saying, 'I have hid my feelings, fearing they should do
    me wrong;'
Saying, 'Dost thou love me, cousin?' weeping, 'I have
    loved thee long.'

Love took up the glass of Time, and turned it in his
    glowing hands;
Every moment, lightly shaken, ran itself in golden
    sands.

Love took up the harp of Life, and smote on all the
    chords with might;
Smote the chord of Self, that, trembling, passed in
    music out of sight.

Many a morning on the moorland did we hear the
    copses ring,
And her whisper thronged my pulses with the fullness
    of the Spring.

Many an evening by the waters did we watch the stately
    ships,
And our spirits rushed together at the touching of the
    lips.

O my cousin, shallow-hearted! O my Amy, mine no
    more!
O the dreary, dreary moorland! O the barren, barren
    shore!

Falser than all fancy fathoms, falser than all songs have
    sung,
Puppet to a father's threat, and servile to a shrewish
    tongue!

Is it well to wish thee happy? – having known me – to
    decline
On a range of lower feelings and a narrower heart than
    mine!

Yet it shall be; thou shalt lower to his level day by day,
What is fine within thee growing coarse to sympathise
    with clay.

As the husband is, the wife is: thou art mated with a
    clown,
And the grossness of his nature will have weight to drag
    thee down.

He will hold thee, when his passion shall have spent its
    novel force,
Something better than his dog, a little dearer than his
    horse.

What is this? his eyes are heavy: think not they are
    glazed with wine.
Go to him: it is thy duty: take his hand in thine.

It may be my lord is weary, that his brain is
    overwrought:
Soothe him with thy finer fancies, touch him with thy
    lighter thought.

He will answer to the purpose, easy things to
    understand –
Better thou wert dead before me, though I slew thee
    with my hand!

Better thou and I were lying, hidden from the heart's
    disgrace,
Rolled in one another's arms, and silent in a last
    embrace.

Cursèd be the social wants that sin against the strength
    of youth!
Cursèd be the social lies that warp us from the living
    truth!

Cursèd be the sickly forms that err from honest Nature's
    rule!
Cursèd be the gold that gilds the straitened forehead of
    the fool!

Well – 'tis well that I should bluster! – Hadst thou less
    unworthy proved –
Would to God – for I had loved thee more than ever
    wife was loved.

Am I mad, that I should cherish that which bears but
    bitter fruit?
I will pluck it from my bosom, though my heart be at
    the root.

Never, though my mortal summers to such lengths of
    years should come
As the many-wintered crow that leads the clanging
    rookery home.

Where is comfort? in division of the records of the
  mind?
Can I part her from herself, and love her, as I knew her,
  kind?

I remember one that perished: sweetly did she speak
  and move:
Such a one do I remember, whom to look at was to
  love.

Can I think of her as dead, and love her for the love she
  bore?
No – she never loved me truly: love is love for evermore.

Comfort? comfort scorned of devils! this is truth the
  poet sings,
That a sorrow's crown of sorrow is remembering
  happier things.

Alfred, Lord Tennyson

The Chess-Board

Irene, do you yet remember
Ere we were grown so sadly wise,
Those evenings in the bleak December,
Curtained warm from the snowy weather,
When you and I played chess together,
Checkmated by each other's eyes?
Ah, still I see your soft white hand
Hovering warm o'er queen and knight,
Brave pawns in valiant battle stand:
The double castles guard the wings;
The bishop, bent on distant things,
Moves, sidling, through the fight,
Our fingers touch; our glances meet,

And falter; falls your golden hair
Against my cheek; your bosom sweet
Is heaving. Down the field, your queen
Rides slow her soldiery all between,
And checks me unaware.

Ah me! the little battle's done,
Dispersed is all its chivalry;
Full many a move, since then, have we
'Mid life's perplexing chequers made,
And many a game with fortune played, –
What is it we have won?
This, this at least – if this alone; –
That never, never, never more,
As in those old still nights of yore,
(Ere we were grown so sadly wise)
Can you and I shut out the skies,
Shut out the world, and wintry weather,
And, eyes exchanging warmth with eyes,
Play chess, as then we played, together!

Edward Robert Bulwer Lytton, First Earl of Lytton

Is It A Month?

Is it a month since I and you
In the starlight of Glen Dubh
Stretched beneath a hazel bough
Kissed from ear and throat to brow,
Since your fingers, neck and chin
Made the bars that fenced me in,
Till Paradise seemed but a wreck
Near your bosom, brow and neck
And stars grew wilder, growing wise,
In the splendour of your eyes!
Since the weasel wandered near

Whilst we kissed from ear to ear
And the wet and wildered leaves
Blew about your cap and sleeves,
Till the moon sank tired through the ledge
Of the wet and wintry hedge?
And we took the starry lane
Back to Dublin town again.

J. M. Synge

Is It Indeed So?
(Sonnets From the Portuguese XXIII)

Is it indeed so! If I lay here dead,
Wouldst thou miss any life in losing mine?
And would the sun for thee more coldly shine,
Because of grave-damps falling round my head?
I marvelled, my Belovèd, when I read
Thy thought so in the letter. I am thine –
But . . . *so* much to thee? Can I pour thy wine
While my hands tremble? Then my soul, instead
Of dreams of death, resumes life's lower range.
Then, love me, Love! look on me . . . breathe on me!
As brighter ladies do not count it strange,
For love, to give up acres and degree,
I yield the grave for thy sake, and exchange
My near sweet view of Heaven, for earth with thee!

Elizabeth Barrett Browning

Duet

(From Becket)

Is it the wind of the dawn that I hear in the pine
    overhead?
No; but the voice of the deep as it hollows the
    cliffs of the land.
Is there a voice coming up with the voice of the
    deep from the strand,
One coming up with a song in the flush of the
    glimmering red?
Love that is born of the deep coming up with
    the sun from the sea.
Love that can shape or can shatter a life till the
    life shall have fled?
Nay, let us welcome him, Love that can lift up
    a life from the dead.
Keep him away from the lone little isle.
Let us be, let us be.
Nay, let him make it his own, let him reign in
    it – he, it is he,
Love that is born of the deep coming up with
    the sun from the sea.

Alfred, Lord Tennyson

Farewell

It is buried and done with
The love that we knew:
Those cobwebs we spun with
Are beaded with dew.

I loved thee; I leave thee:
To love thee was pain:
I dare not believe thee
To love thee again.

Like spectres unshriven
Are the years that I lost;
To thee they were given
Without count of cost.

I cannot revive them
By penance or prayer;
Hell's tempest must drive them
Through turbulent air.

Farewell, and forget me:
For I too am free
From the shame that beset me,
The sorrow of thee.

John Addington Symonds

A Right Pithy Song

It is not Beauty I demand,
A crystal brow, the moon's despair,
Nor the snow's daughter, a white hand,
Nor mermaid's yellow pride of hair.

Tell me not of your starry eyes,
Your lips that seem on roses fed,
Your breasts where Cupid trembling lies,
Nor sleeps for kissing of his bed.

A bloomy pair of vermeil cheeks,
Like Hebe's in her ruddiest hours,
A breath that softer music speaks
Than summer winds a-wooing flowers.

These are but gauds; nay, what are lips?
Coral beneath the ocean-stream,

Whose brink when your adventurer sips
Full oft he perisheth on them.

And what are cheeks but ensigns oft
That wave hot youth to fields of blood?
Did Helen's breast though ne'er so soft,
Do Greece or Ilium any good?

Eyes can with baleful ardor burn,
Poison can breath that erst perfumed,
There's many a white hand holds an urn
With lovers' hearts to dust consumed.

For crystal brows – there's naught within,
They are but empty cells for pride;
He who the Syren's hair would win
Is mostly strangled in the tide.

Give me, instead of beauty's bust,
A tender heart, a loyal mind,
Which with temptation I could trust,
Yet never linked with error find.

One in whose gentle bosom I
Could pour my secret heart of woes,
Like the care-burdened honey-fly
That hides his murmurs in the rose.

My earthly comforter! whose love
So indefeasible might be,
That when my spirit won above
Hers could not stay for sympathy.

George Darley

Youth And Art

It once might have been, once only:
We lodged in a street together,
You, a sparrow on the housetop lonely,
I, a lone she-bird of his feather.

Your trade was with sticks and clay,
You thumbed, thrust, patted and polished,
Then laughed 'They will see some day
'Smith made, and Gibson demolished.'

My business was song, song, song;
I chirped, cheeped, trilled and twittered,
'Kate Brown's on the boards ere long,
'And Grisi's existence embittered!'

I earned no more by a warble
Than you by a sketch in plaster;
You wanted a piece of marble,
I needed a music-master.

We studied hard in our styles,
Chipped each at a crust like Hindoos,
For air looked out on the tiles,
For fun watched each other's windows.

You lounged, like a boy of the South,
Cap and blouse – nay, a bit of beard too;
Or you got it, rubbing your mouth
With fingers the clay adhered to.

And I – soon managed to find
Weak points in the flower-fence facing,
Was forced to put up a blind
And be safe in my corset-lacing.

No harm! It was not my fault
If you never turned your eye's tail up
As I shook upon E *in alt*,
Or ran the chromatic scale up:

For spring bade the sparrows pair,
And the boys and girls gave guesses,
And stalls in our street looked rare
With bulrush and watercresses.

Why did not you pinch a flower
In a pellet of clay and fling it?
Why did not I put a power
Of thanks in a look, or sing it?

I did look, sharp as a lynx,
(And yet the memory rankles)
When models arrived, some minx
Tripped up-stairs, she and her ankles.

But I think I gave you as good!
'That foreign fellow, – who can know
How she pays, in a playful mood,
For his tuning her that piano?'

Could you say so, and never say
'Suppose we join hands and fortunes,
And I fetch her from over the way,
Her, piano, and long tunes and short tunes?'

No, no: you would not be rash,
Nor I rasher and something over:
You've to settle yet Gibson's hash,
And Grisi yet lives in clover.

But you meet the Prince at the Board,
I'm queen myself at *bals-paré*
I've married a rich old lord,
And you're dubbed knight and an R.A.

Each life unfulfilled, you see;
It hangs still, patchy and scrappy:
We have not sighed deep, laughed free,
Starved, feasted, despaired, – been happy.

And nobody calls you a dunce,
And people suppose me clever:
This could but have happened once,
And we missed it, lost it for ever.

Robert Browning

Time Of Roses

It was not in the Winter
Our loving lot was cast;
It was the time of roses –
We plucked them as we passed!

That churlish season never frowned
On early lovers yet:
O no – the world was newly crowned
With flowers when first we met!

'Twas twilight, and I bade you go,
But still you held me fast;
It was the time of roses –
We plucked them as we passed!

Thomas Hood

Departure

It was not like your great and gracious ways!
Do you, that have naught other to lament,
Never, my Love, repent
Of how, that July afternoon,
You went,
With sudden, unintelligible phrase,
And frightened eye,
Upon your journey of so many days
Without a single kiss, or a good-bye?
I knew, indeed, that you were parting soon;
And so we sate, within the low sun's rays,
You whispering to me, for your voice was weak,
Your harrowing praise.
Well, it was well
To hear you such things speak,
And I could tell
What made your eyes a growing gloom of love,
As a warm South-wind sombres a March grove.
And it was like your great and gracious ways
To turn your talk on daily things, my Dear,
Lifting the luminous, pathetic lash
To let the laughter flash,
Whilst I drew near,
Because you spoke so low that I could scarcely hear.
But all at once to leave me at the last,
More at the wonder than the loss aghast,
With huddled, unintelligible phrase,
And frightened eye,
And go your journey of all days
With not one kiss, or a good-bye,
And the only loveless look the look with which you
    passed:
'Twas all unlike your great and gracious ways.

Coventry Patmore

The Haven

It was not love, but o'er the array
Of maiden faces clustering there
My glance careered, which well might stay,
For this was frank and that was fair.

No haven for my sail that drove,
No pharos; sunniest isles I passed;
Then suddenly – it was not love –
The haven, and an anchor cast.

Edward Dowden

Kissing Her Hair

Kissing her hair I sat against her feet,
Wove and unwove it, wound and found it sweet;
Made fast therewith her hands, drew down her eyes,
Deep as deep flowers and dreamy like dim skies;
With her own tresses bound and found her fair,
Kissing her hair.

Sleep were no sweeter than her face to me,
Sleep of cold sea-bloom under the cold sea;
What pain could get between my face and hers?
What new sweet thing would love not relish worse?
Unless, perhaps, white death had kissed me there,
Kissing her hair?

Algernon Charles Swinburne

Sonnet

Lady, whom my belovéd loves so well!
When on his clasping arm thy head reclineth,
When on thy lips his ardent kisses dwell,
And the bright flood of burning light that shineth
In his dark eyes, is poured into thine;
When thou shalt lie enfolded to his heart
In all the trusting helplessness of love;
If in such joy sorrow can find a part,
Oh, give one sigh unto a doom like mine!
Which I would have thee pity, but not prove.
One cold, calm, careless, wintry look that fell
Haply by chance on one, is all that he
Ever gave my love; round that, my wild thoughts dwell
In one eternal pang of memory.

Fanny Kemble

Non Sum Qualis Eram Bonae Sub Regno Cynarae

Last night, ah, yesternight, betwixt her lips and mine
There fell thy shadow, Cynara! thy breath was shed
Upon my soul between the kisses and the wine;
And I was desolate and sick of an old passion,
Yea, I was desolate and bowed my head:
I have been faithful to thee, Cynara! in my fashion.

All night upon mine heart I felt her warm heart beat,
Night-long within mine arms in love and sleep she lay;
Surely the kisses of her bought red mouth were sweet;
But I was desolate and sick of an old passion,
When I awoke and found the dawn was gray:
I have been faithful to thee, Cynara! in my fashion.

I have forgot much, Cynara! gone with the wind,
Flung roses, roses riotously with the throng,
Dancing, to put thy pale, lost lilies out of mind;

But I was desolate and sick of an old passion,
Yea, all the time, because the dance was long:
I have been faithful to thee, Cynara! in my fashion.

I cried for madder music and for stronger wine,
But when the feast is finished and the lamps expire,
Then falls thy shadow, Cynara! the night is thine;
And I am desolate and sick of an old passion,
Yea hungry for the lips of my desire:
I have been faithful to thee, Cynara! in my fashion.

Ernest Dowson

Barcarolle

Last night we sailed, my love and I,
Last night and years ago –
Was it moon or sea, we drifted through?
I think I shall never know!
We had no oar –
We neared no shore –
We floated with the tide;
The moon was white,
And the sea alight,
And none in the world beside.

I and my love, we said farewell –
It is years and years away.
We kissed our last in a life gone by –
I think it was yesterday!
Oh! for heaven, give me
A moon and a sea
To sail, when we both have died,
With never an oar –
With never a shore –
Drifting on with the tide!

May Probyn

Marriage Morning
(From The Window)

Light, so low upon earth,
You send a flash to the sun.
Here is the golden close of love,
All my wooing is done.
Oh, the woods and the meadows,
Woods where we hid from the wet,
Stiles where we stayed to be kind,
Meadows in which we met!

Light, so low in the vale
You flash and lighten afar,
For this is the golden morning of love,
And you are his morning star.
Flash, I am coming, I come,
By meadow and stile and wood,
Oh, lighten into my eyes and heart,
Into my heart and my blood!

Heart, are you great enough
For a love that never tires?
O heart, are you great enough for love?
I have heard of thorns and briers.
Over the thorns and briers,
Over the meadows and stiles,
Over the world to the end of it
Flash for a million miles.

Alfred, Lord Tennyson

Like a Drop of Water is My Heart
(From Youth and Maidenhead

Like a drop of water is my heart
Laid upon her soft and rosy palm,
Turned whichever way her hand doth turn,
Trembling in an ecstasy of calm.
Like a broken rose-leaf is my heart,
Held within her close and burning clasp
Breathing only dying sweetness out,
Withering beneath the fat grasp.

Like a vapoury cloudlet is my heart,
Growing into beauty near the sun,
Gaining rainbow hues in her embrace,
Melting into tears when it is done.

Like mine own dear harp is this my heart,
Dumb, without the hand that sweeps its strings;
Though the hand be careless or be cruel,
When it comes, my heart breaks forth and sings.

Sarah Williams

Lo, My Loved Is Dying

Lo, my loved is dying, and the call
Is come that I must die,
All the leaves are dying, all
Dying, drifting by.
Every leaf is lonely in its fall,
Every flower has its speck and stain;
The birds from hedge and tree
Lisp mournfully,
And the great reconciliation of this pain
Lies in the full, soft rain.

Michael Field

For an Epitaph at Fiesole

Lo! where the four mimosas blend their shade,
In calm repose at last is Landor laid;
For ere he slept he saw them planted here
By her his soul had ever held most dear,
And he had lived enough when he had dried her tear.

Walter Savage Landor

The Flight

Look back with longing eyes and know that I will
    follow,
Lift me up in your love as a light wing lifts a swallow,
Let our flight be far in sun or blowing rain –
But what if I heard my first love calling me again?

Hold me on your heart as the brave sea holds the foam,
Take me far away to the hills that hide your home:
Peace shall thatch the roof and love shall latch the door –
But what if I heard my first love calling me again?

Sara Teasdale

A Superscription
(From The House Of Life. Sonnet XCVII)

Look in my face; my name is Might-have-been;
I am also called No-more, Too-late, Farewell;
Unto thine ear I hold the dead-sea shell
Cast up thy Life's foam-fretted feet between;
Unto thine eyes the glass where that is seen
Which had Life's form and Love's, but by my spell
Is now a shaken shadow intolerable,
Of ultimate things unuttered the frail screen.

Mark me, how still I am! But should there dart
One moment through thy soul the soft surprise
Of that winged Peace which lulls the breath of sighs, –
Then shalt thou see me smile, and turn apart
Thy visage to mine ambush at thy heart
Sleepless with cold commemorative eyes.

Dante Gabriel Rossetti

In Memoriam CXXVI

Love is and was my Lord and King,
And in his presence I attend
To hear the tidings of my friend,
Which every hour his couriers bring.

Love is and was my King and Lord,
And will be, though as yet I keep
Within his court on earth, and sleep
Encompassed by his faithful guard,

And hear at times a sentinel
Who moves about from place to place,
And whispers to the worlds of space,
In the deep night, that all is well.

Alfred, Lord Tennyson

Love Is Enough

Love is enough: though the World be a-waning,
And the woods have no voice but the voice of
     complaining,
Though the sky be too dark for dim eyes to discover
The gold-cups and daisies fair blooming thereunder,
Though the hills be held shadows, and the sea a dark
     wonder,
And this day draw a veil over all deeds passed over,
Yet their hands shall not tremble, their feet shall not
     falter;
The void shall not weary, the fear shall not alter
These lips and these eyes of the loved and the lover.

William Morris

Pastiche

Love, oh, love's a dainty sweeting,
Wooing now, and now retreating;
Brightest joy and blackest care,
Swift as light, and light as air.

Would you seize and fix and capture
All his evanescent rapture?
Bind him fast with golden curls,
Fetter with a chain of pearls?

Would you catch him in a net,
Like a white moth prankt with jet.
Clutch him, and his bloomy wing
Turns a dead, discoloured thing!

Pluck him like a rosebud red,
And he leaves a thorn instead;
Let him go without a care,
And he follows unaware.

Love, oh, Love's a dainty sweeting,
Wooing now, and now retreating;
Lightly come, and lightly gone,
Lost when most securely won!

Mathilde Blind

Beyond

Love's aftermath! I think the time is now
That we must gather in, alone, apart
The saddest crop of all the crops that grow,
Love's aftermath.
Ah, sweet, – sweet yesterday, the tears that start
Can not put back the dial, this is, I trow,
Our harvesting! Thy kisses chill my heart,
Our lips are cold; averted eyes avow
The twilight of poor love: we can but part
Dumbly and sadly, reaping as we sow,
Love's aftermath.

Ernest Dowson

Master In Loving

Master in loving! till we met
I lacked the pattern thy sweet love hath set;
I hear Death's footstep – must we then forget? –
Stay, stay – not yet!

George Eliot

Annie Laurie
(A Victorian Version of the Song)

Maxwellton braes are bonnie,
Where early fa's the dew,
And it's there that Annie Laurie
Gie'd me her promise true;
Gie'd me her promise true
That ne'er forgot sall be,
But for bonnie Annie Laurie
I'd lay doun my head and dee.

Her brow is like the snaw-drift,
Her neck is like the swan,
Her face it is the fairest
That e'er the sun shone on;
That e'er the sun shone on,
And dark blue is her e'e;
And for bonnie Annie Laurie
I'd lay doun my head and dee.

Like dew on the gowan lying
Is the fa' o' her fairy feet;
And like winds in summer sighing
Her voice is low and sweet;
Her voice is low and sweet,
And she's a' the world to me,
And for bonnie Annie Laurie
I'd lay doun my head and dee.

Lady John Scott

On The Doorstep

Midnight long is over-past
As we loiter, and the rain falls fast,
As we loiter on your doorstep,
And the rain falls fast.

Will the watchful mother hear,
As we whisper, is your mother near,
Keeping there behind the curtain
An attentive ear?

But we have much to say,
As we linger, ere I go my way,
In the dark upon your doorstep,
We could talk till day.

There is no-one in the street
As I hold you in my arms, my sweet
As I kiss you on your doorstep,
As I kiss you for good-night, my sweet.

Arthur Symons

From Sappho

Mother, I cannot mind my wheel;
My fingers ache, my lips are dry:
Oh! if you felt the pain I feel!
But Oh, who ever felt as I?

No longer could I doubt him true;
All other men may use deceit:
He always said my eyes were blue,
And often swore my lips were sweet.

Walter Savage Landor

Song Of The Forsaken

My cheek is faded sair, love,
An' lichtless fa's my e'e;
My breast a' lane and bare, love,
Has aye a bield for thee.
My breast, though lane and bare,
The hame o' cauld despair,
Yet ye've a dwallin' there,
A' darksome though it be.

Yon guarded roses glowin',
It's wha daur mint to pu'?
But aye the wee bit gowan
Ilk reckless hand may strew.
An' aye the wee, wee gowan,
Unsheltered, lanely growin',
Unkent, uncared its ruin,
Sae marklessly it grew.

An' am I left to rue, then,
Wha ne'er kent Love but thee;
An' gae a love as true, then,
As woman's heart can gie?
But can ye cauldly view,
A bosom burstin' fu'?
An' hae ye broken noo,
The heart ye *sought* frae me?

William Thom

My Delight And Thy Delight

My delight and thy delight,
Walking, like two angels white,
In the gardens of the night:

My desire and thy desire
Twining to a tongue of fire,
Leaping live, and laughing higher;

Through the everlasting strife
In the mystery of life.

Love, from whom the world begun,
Hath the secret of the sun.

Love can tell, and love alone,
Whence the million stars were strewn,
Why each atom knows its own,
How, in spite of woe and death,
Gay is life, and sweet is breath:

This he taught us, this we knew,
Happy in his science true,
Hand in hand as we stood
'Neath the shadows of the wood,
Heart to heart as we lay
In the dawning of the day.

Robert Bridges

My Grief On The Sea
(From the Irish)

My grief on the sea,
How the waves of it roll!
For they heave between me
And the love of my soul!

Abandoned, forsaken,
To grief and to care,
Will the sea ever waken
Relief from despair?

My grief and my trouble!
Were he and I were
In the province of Leinster,
Or county of Clare.

Were I and my darling –
Oh, heart-bitter wound! –
On board of the ship
For America bound.

On a green bed of rushes
All last night I lay,
And I flung it abroad
With the heat of the day.

And my love came behind me –
He came from the South;
His breast to my bosom,
His mouth to my mouth.

Douglas Hyde

A Birthday

My heart is like a singing bird
Whose nest is in a watered shoot;
My heart is like an apple tree
Whose boughs are bent with thick-set fruit;
My heart is like a rainbow shell
That paddles in a halcyon sea;
My heart is gladder than all these,
Because my love is come to me.

Raise me a dais of silk and down;
Hang it with vair and purple dyes;
Carve it in doves and pomegranates,
And peacocks with a hundred eyes;
Work it in gold and silver grapes,
In leaves and silver fleur-de-lys;
Because the birthday of my life
Is come, my love is come to me.

Christina Rossetti

The Wind Bloweth Where It Listeth

My heart lies light in my own breast
That yesterday in yours found rest.

Indeed beloved I would stay
With you today as yesterday;

But oh! the being comes and goes,
The spirit is a wind that blows.

Though lip to lip no more we press
Our spirits feel that tenderness

That woke within us here and fled
To its own heaven overhead.

It sits there in a starry place,
With looks of longing on its face,

And beckons us to mount and find
The love that fled upon the wind.

Not the old wayward child to see
But some bright-haired divinity.

Susan Mitchell

The Garden

My heart shall be thy garden. Come my own,
Into thy garden; thine be happy hours
Among my fairest thoughts, my tallest flowers,
From root to crowning petal thine alone.
Thine is the place, from where the seeds are sown
Up to the sky enclosed, with all its showers.

But ah, the birds, the birds! Who shall build bowers
To keep these thine? O friend, the birds have flown.
For as these come and go, and quit our pine
To follow the sweet season, or, new-comers,
Sing one song only from our alder-trees,
My heart has thoughts, which, though thine eyes hold
    mine,
Flit to the silent world and other summers,
With wings that dip beyond the silver seas.

Alice Meynell

First Love

My long first year of perfect love,
My deep new dream of joy;
She was a little chubby girl,
I was a chubby boy.

I wore a crimson frock, white drawers,
A belt, a crown was on it;
She wore some angel's kind of dress
And such a tiny bonnet,

Old-fashioned, but the soft brown hair
Would never keep its place;
A little maid with violet eyes,
And sunshine in her face.

O my child-queen, in those lost days
How sweet was daily living!
How humble and how proud I grew,
How rich by merely giving!

She went to school, the parlour-maid
Slow stepping to her trot;
That parlour-maid, ah, did she feel
How lofty was her lot!

Across the road I saw her lift
My Queen, and with a sigh
I envied Raleigh; my new coat
Was hung a peg too high.

A hoard of never-given gifts
I cherished, – priceless pelf;
'Twas two whole days ere I devoured
That peppermint myself.

In Church I only prayed for her –
'O God bless Lucy Hill;'
Child, may His angels keep their arms
Ever around you still.

But when the hymn came round, with heart
That feared some heart's surprising
Its secret sweet, I climbed the seat
'Mid rustling and uprising;

And there against her mother's arm
The sleeping child was leaning,
While far away the hymn went on,
The music and the meaning.

Oh I loved with more of pain
Since then, with more of passion,
Loved with the aching in my love
After our grown-up fashion;

Yet could I almost be content
To lose here at your feet
A year or two, you murmuring elm,
To dream a dream so sweet.

Edward Dowden

White An' Blue

My love is o' comely height, an' straight,
An' comely in all her ways an' gait,
In feäce she do show the rwose's hue,
An' her lids on her eyes be white on blue.

When Elemley clubmen walked in Maÿ
An' vo'k come in clusters, every waÿ,
As soon as the zun dried up the dew,
An' clouds in the sky wer white on blue,

She come by the down, wi' trippen walk,
By deäisies, an' sheenen banks o' chalk,
An' brooks, where the crowvoot flowers did strew
The sky-tinted water, white on blue.

She nodded her head, as plaÿed the band;
She dapped wi' her voot, as she did stand;
She danced in a reel, a-wearen new
A skirt wi' a jacket, white wi' blue.

I singled her out vrom thin an' stout,
Vrom slender an' stout I chose her out;
An' what, in the evenen, could I do,
But gie her my breast-knot, white an' blue?

William Barnes

The Churchyard On The Sands

My Love lies in the gates of foam,
The last dear wreck of shore;
The naked sea-marsh binds her home,
The sand her chamber door.

The gray gull flaps the written stones,
The ox-birds chase the tide;
And near that narrow field of bones
Great ships at anchor ride.

Black piers with crust of dripping green,
One foreland, like a hand,
O'er intervals of grass between
Dim lonely dunes of sand.

A church of silent weathered looks,
A breezy reddish tower,
A yard whose mounded resting-nooks
Are tinged with sorrel flower.

In peace the swallow's eggs are laid
Along the belfry walls;
The tempest does not reach her shade,
The rain her silent halls.

But sails are sweet in summer sky,
The lark throws down a lay;
The long salt levels steam and dry,
The cloud-heart melts away.

But patches of the sea-pink shine,
The pied crows poise and come;
The mallow hangs, the bindweeds twine,
Where her sweet lips are dumb.

The passion of the wave is mute;
No sound or ocean shock;
No music save the rilling flute
That marks the curlew flock.

But yonder when the wind is keen,
And rainy air is clear,
The merchant city's spires are seen,
The toil of men grows near.

Along the coast-way grind the wheels
Of endless carts of coal;
And on the sides of giant keels
The shipyard hammers roll.

The world creeps here upon the shout,
And stirs my heart in pain;
The mist descends and blots it out,
And I am strong again.

Strong and alone, my dove, with thee;
And, though mine eyes be wet,
There's nothing in the world to me
So dear as my regret.

I would not change my sorrow, sweet,
For others' nuptial hours;
I love the daisies at thy feet
More than their orange flowers.

My hand alone shall tend thy tomb
From leaf-bud to leaf-fall,
And wreathe around each season's bloom
Till autumn ruins all.

Let snowdrops, early in the year,
Droop o'er her silent breast;
And bid the later cowslip rear
The amber of its crest.

Come hither, linnets tufted-red,
Drift by, O wailing tern;
Set pure vale lilies at her head,
At her feet lady-fern.

Grow, samphire, at the tidal brink,
Wave, pansies of the shore,
To whisper how alone I think
Of her for evermore.

Bring blue sea-hollies thorny, keen,
Long lavender in flower;
Gray wormwood like a hoary queen,
Stanch mullein like a tower.

O sea-wall mounded long and low
Let iron bounds be thine;
Nor let the salt wave overflow
That breast I held divine.

Nor float its sea-weed to her hair,
Nor dim her eyes with sands:
No fluted cockle burrow where
Sleep folds her patient hands.

Though thy crest feel the wild sea's breath,
Though tide-weight tear thy root,
Oh, guard the treasure house, where Death
Has bound my darling mute.

Though cold her pale lips to reward
With love's own mysteries,
Ah, rob no daisy from her sward,
Rough gale of eastern seas!

Ah, render sere no silent bent,
That by her head-stone waves;
Let noon and golden summer blent
Pervade these ocean graves.

And, ah, dear heart, in thy still nest,
Resign this earth of woes,
Forget the ardours of the west,
Neglect the morning glows.

Sleep, and forget all things but one,
Heard in each wave of sea, –
How lonely all the years will run
Until I rest by thee.

John Leicester Warren, Lord De Tabley

Sunday Up The River

My love o'er the water bends dreaming;
It glideth and glideth away:
She sees there her own beauty, gleaming
Through shadow and ripple and spray.

O tell her thou murmuring river,
As past her your light wavelets roll,
How steadfast that image for ever
Shines pure in pure depths of my soul.

James Thomson

The Leper

*(Based upon the story of Yolande de Sallières recounted in
the Grandes Chroniques de France (1505))*

Nothing is better, I well think,
Than love; the hidden well-water
Is not so delicate to drink:
This was well seen of me and her.

I served her in a royal house;
I served her wine and curious meat.
For will to kiss between her brows
I had no heart to sleep or eat.

Mere scorn God knows she had of me;
A poor scribe, nowise great or fair,
Who plucked his clerk's hood back to see
Her curled-up lips and amorous hair.

I vex my head with thinking this.
Yea, though God always hated me,
And hates me now that I can kiss
Her eyes, plait up her hair to see

How she then wore it on the brows,
Yet am I glad to have her dead
Here in this wretched wattled house
Where I can kiss her eyes and head.

Nothing is better, I well know,
Than love; no amber in cold sea
Or gathered berries under snow:
That is well seen of her and me.

Three thoughts I make my pleasure of:
First I take heart and think of this:
That knight's gold hair she chose to love,
His mouth she had such will to kiss.

Then I remember that sundawn
I brought him by a privy way
Out at her lattice, and thereon
What gracious words she found to say.

(Cold rushes for such little feet –
Both feet could lie into my hand.
A marvel was it of my sweet
Her upright body could so stand.)

'Sweet friend, God give you thank and grace;
Now am I clean and whole of shame,
Nor shall men burn me in the face
For my sweet fault that scandals them.'

I tell you over word by word.
She, sitting edgewise on her bed,
Holding her feet, said thus. The third,
A sweeter thing than these, I said.

God, that makes time and ruins it,
And alters not, abiding God,
Changed with disease her body sweet,
The body of love wherein she abode.

Love is more sweet and comelier
Than a dove's throat strained out to sing.
All they spat out and cursed at her
And cast her forth for a base thing.

They cursed her, seeing how God had wrought
This curse to plague her, a curse of his.
Fools were they surely, seeing not
How sweeter than all sweet she is.

He that had held her by the hair,
With kissing lips blinding her eyes.
Felt her bright bosom, strained and bare,
Sigh under him, with short mad cries

Out of her throat and sobbing mouth
And body broken up with love,
With sweet hot tears his lips were loth
Her own should taste the savour of,

Yea, he inside whose grasp all night
Her fervent body leapt or lay,
Stained with sharp kisses red and white,
Found her a plague to spurn away.

I hid her in this wattled house,
I served her water and poor bread.
For joy to kiss between her brows
Time upon time I was nigh dead.

Bread failed; we got but well-water
And gathered grass with dropping seed.
I had such joy of kissing her,
I had small care to sleep or feed.

Sometimes when service made me glad
The sharp tears leapt between my lids,
Falling on her, such joy I had
To do the service God forbids.

'I pray you let me be at peace,
Get hence, make room for me to die.'
She said that: her poor lip would cease,
Put up to mine, and turn to cry.

I said, 'Bethink yourself how love
Fared in us twain, what either did;
Shall I unclothe my soul thereof?
That I should do this, God forbid.'

Yea, though God hateth us, he knows
That hardly in a little thing
Love faileth of the work it does
Till it grow ripe for gathering.

Six months, and now my sweet is dead
A trouble takes me; I know not
If all were done well, all well said,
No word or tender deed forgot.

Too sweet, for the least part in her,
To have shed life out by fragments; yet,
Could the close mouth catch breath and stir,
I might see something I forget.

Six months, and I sit still and hold
In two cold palms of her cold two feet.
Her hair, half grey half ruined gold,
Thrills me and burns me in kissing it.

Love bites and stings me through, to see
Her keen face made of sunken bones,
Her worn-off eyelids madden me,
That were shot through with purple once.

She said, 'Be good with me; I grow
So tired for shame's sake, I shall die
If you say nothing:' even so.
And she is dead now, and shame put by.

Yea, and the scorn she had of me
In the old time doubtless vexed her then.
I never should have kissed her. See
What fools God's anger makes of men!

She might have loved me a little too,
Had I been humbler for her sake.
But that new shame could make love new
She saw not – yet her shame did make.

I took too much upon my love,
Having for such mean service done
Her beauty and all the ways thereof,
Her face and all the sweet thereon.

Yea, all this while I tended her,
I know the old love held fast his part:
I know the old scorn waxed heavier,
Mixed with sad wonder, in her heart.

It may be all my love went wrong –
A scribe's work writ awry and blurred,
Scrawled after the blind evensong –
Spoilt music with no perfect word.

But surely I would fain have done
All things the best I could. Perchance
Because I failed, came short of one,
She kept at heart that other man's.

I am grown blind with all these things:
It may be now she hath in sight
Some better knowledge; still there clings
The old question. Will not God do right?

Algernon Charles Swinburne

Summer Night

(From The Princess)

Now sleeps the crimson petal, now the white;
Nor waves the cypress in the palace walk;
Nor winks the gold fin in the porphyry font:
The firefly wakens: waken thou with me.

Now droops the milk-white peacock like a ghost,
And like a ghost she glimmers on to me.

Now lies the Earth all Danaë to the stars,
And all thy heart lies open unto me.

Now slides the silent meteor on, and leaves
A shining furrow, as thy thoughts in me.

Now folds the lily all her sweetness up,
And slips into the bosom of the lake;
So fold thyself, my dearest, thou, and slip
Into my bosom and be lost in me.

Alfred, Lord Tennyson

The Revenant

O all ye fair ladies with your colours and your graces,
And your eyes clear in flame of candle and hearth,
Toward the dark of this old window lift not up your
    smiling faces,
Where a Shade stands forlorn from the cold of the
    earth.

God knows I could not rest for one I still was thinking
    of;
Like a rose sheathed in beauty her spirit was to me;
Now out of unforgottenness a bitter draught I'm
    drinking of,
'Tis sad of such beauty unremembered to be.

Men all are shades, O Women. Winds wist not of the
    way they blow
Apart from your kindness, life's at best but a snare.
Though a tongue, now past praise, this bitter thing doth
    say, I know
What solitude means, and how, homeless, I fare.

Strange, strange, are ye all – except in beauty shared
    with her –
Since I seek one I loved, yet was faithless to in death.
Not life enough I heaped, so thus my heart must fare
    with her,
Now wrapt in the gross clay, bereft of life's breath.

Walter De La Mare

Chamber Music **XVI**

O cool is the valley now
And there, love, will we go
For many a choir is singing now
Where Love did sometime go.
And hear you not the thrushes calling,
Calling us away?
O cool and pleasant is the valley
And there, love, will we stay.

James Joyce

Grief Of A Girl's Heart

(From the Irish)

O Donal Oge, if you go across the sea,
Bring myself with you and do not forget it;
And you will have a sweetheart for fair days and market
    days,
And the daughter of the King of Greece beside you at
    night.

It is late last night the dog was speaking of you;
The snipe was speaking of you in her deep marsh.
It is you are the lonely bird through the woods;
And that you may be without a mate until you find me.

You promised me, and you said a lie to me,
That you would be before me where the sheep are
    flocked;
I gave a whistle and three hundred cries to you,
And I found nothing there but a bleating lamb.

You promised me a thing that was hard for you,
A ship of gold under a silver mast;
Twelve towns with a market in all of them,
And a fine white court by the side of the sea.

You promised me a thing that is not possible,
That you would give me gloves of the skin of a fish;
That you would give me shoes of the skin of a bird;
And a suit of the dearest silk in Ireland.

O Donal Oge, it is I would be better to you
Than a high, proud, spendthrift lady:
I would milk the cow; I would bring help to you;
And if you were hard pressed, I would strike a blow for
    you.

O, ochone, and it's not with hunger
Or with wanting food, or drink, or sleep,
That I am growing thin, and my life is shortened;
But it is the love of a young man has withered me away.

It is early in the morning that I saw him coming,
Going along the road on the back of a horse;
He did not come to me; he made nothing of me;
And it is on my way home that I cried my fill.

When I go by myself to the Well of Loneliness,
I sit down and I go through my trouble;
When I see the world and do not see my boy.
He that has an amber shade in his hair.

It was on that Sunday I gave my love to you;
The Sunday that is last before Easter Sunday.
And myself on my knees reading the Passion;
And my two eyes giving love to you for ever.

O, aya! my mother, give myself to him;
And give him all that you have in the world;
Get out yourself to ask for alms,
And do not come back and forward looking for me.

My mother said to me not to be talking with you,
    to-day,
Or to-morrow, or on Sunday;
It was a bad time she took for telling me that;
It was shutting the door after the house was robbed.

My heart is as black as the blackness of the sloe,
Or as the black coal that is on the smith's forge;
Or as the sole of a shoe left in white halls;
It was you put that darkness over my life.

You have taken the east from me; you have taken the
    west from me,
You have taken what is before me and what is behind
    me;
You have taken the moon, you have taken the sun from
    me,
And my fear is great that you have taken God from me!

Augusta, Lady Gregory

Chamber Music XXXI

O, it was out by Donnycarney
When the bat flew from tree to tree
My love and I did walk together
And sweet were the words she said to me.

Along with us the summer wind
Went murmuring – O, happily! –
But softer than the breath of summer
Was the kiss she gave to me.

James Joyce

O Joy Of Love's Renewing

O joy of love's renewing,
Could love be born again;
Relenting for thy rueing,
And pitying my pain:
O joy of love's awaking.
Could love arise from sleep,
Forgiving our forsaking
The fields we would not reap!

Fleet, fleet we fly, pursuing
The love that fled amain,
But will he list our wooing,
Or call we but in vain?
Ah! vain is all our wooing,
And all our prayers are vain,
Love listeth not our suing,
Love will not wake again.

Andrew Lang

Fatima

O Love, Love, Love! O withering might!
O sun, that from thy noonday height
Shudderest when I strain my sight,
Throbbing through all thy heat and light,
Lo, falling from my constant mind,
Lo, parched and withered, deaf and blind,
I whirl like leaves in roaring wind.

Last night I wasted hateful hours
Below the city's eastern towers:
I thirsted for the brooks, the showers:
I rolled among the tender flowers:
I crushed them on my breast, my mouth;
I looked athwart the burning drouth
Of that long desert to the south.

Last night, when some one spoke his name,
From my swift blood that went and came
A thousand little shafts of flame
Were shivered in my narrow frame.
O Love, O fire! once he drew
With one long kiss my whole soul through
My lips, as sunlight drinketh dew.

Before he mounts the hill, I know
He cometh quickly: from below
Sweet gales, as from deep gardens, blow
Before him, striking on my brow.
In my dry brain my spirit soon,
Down-deepening from swoon to swoon,
Faints like a dazzled morning moon.

The wind sounds like a silver wire,
And from beyond the noon a fire
Is poured upon the hills, and nigher
The skies stoop down in their desire;
And, isled in sudden seas of light,
My heart, pierced through with fierce delight,
Bursts into blossom in his sight.

My whole soul waiting silently,
All naked in a sultry sky,
Droops blinded with his shining eye:
I *will* possess him or will die.
I will grow round him in his place,
Grow, live, die looking on his face,
Die, dying clasped in his embrace.

Alfred, Lord Tennyson

October Tune

O love, turn from the unchanging sea, and gaze
Down these grey slopes upon the year grown old,
A-dying mid the autumn-scented haze
That hangeth o'er the hollow in the wold,
Where the wind-bitten ancient elms infold
Grey church, long barn, orchard, and red-roofed stead,
Wrought in dead days for men a long while dead.

Come down, O love; may not our hands still meet,
Since still we live today, forgetting June,
Forgetting May, deeming October sweet –
– O hearken, hearken! through the afternoon,
The grey tower sings a strange old tinkling tune!
Sweet, sweet, and sad, the toiling year's last breath,
Too satiate of life to strive with death.

And we too – will it not be soft and kind,
That rest from life, from patience and from pain,
That rest from bliss we know not when we find,
That rest from love which ne'er the end can gain? –
– Hark, how the tune swells, that erewhile did wane!
Look up, love! – ah, cling close and never move!
How can I have enough of life and love?

William Morris

O Lyric Love

(From The Ring and the Brook)

O lyric Love, half-angel and half-bird
And all a wonder and a wild desire –
Boldest of hearts that ever braved the sun,
Took sanctuary within the holiest blue,
And sang a kindred soul out to his face, –
Yet human at the red-ripe of the heart –
When the first summons from the darkling earth
Reached thee amid thy chambers, blanched their blue,
And bared them of the glory – to drop down,
To toil for man, to suffer or to die, –
This is the same voice: can thy soul know change?
Hail then, and hearken from the realms of help!
Never may I commence my song, my due
To God who best taught song by gift of thee,
Except with bent head and beseeching hand –

That still, despite the distance and the dark,
What was, again may be; some interchange
Of grace, some splendour once thy very thought,
Some benediction, anciently thy smile:
Never conclude, but raising hand and head
Thither where eyes, that cannot reach, yet yearn
For all hope, all sustainment, all reward,
Their utmost up and on, – so blessing back
In those thy realms of help, that heaven thy home,
Some whiteness which, I judge, thy face makes proud,
Some wanness where, I think, thy foot may fall.

Robert Browning

The Outlaw Of Loch Lene

O many a day have I made good ale in the glen,
That came not of stream, or malt, like the brewing of
  men.
My bed was the ground, my roof, the greenwood above,
And the wealth that I sought – one far kind glance from
  my love.

Alas! on that night when the horses I drove from the
  field,
That I was not near from terror my angel to shield.
She stretched forth her arms, – her mantle she flung to
  the wind,
And swam o'er Loch Lene, her outlawed lover to find.

O would that a freezing sleet-winged tempest did
  sweep,
And I and my love were alone far off on the deep!
I'd ask not a ship, or a bark, or pinnace to save, –
With her hand round my waist, I'd fear not the wind or
  the wave.

'Tis down by the lake where the wild tree fringes its
    sides,
The maid of my heart, the fair one of Heaven resides –
I think as at eve she wanders its mazes along,
The birds go to sleep by the sweet wild twist of her
    song.

Jeremiah Joseph Callanan

Will Ladislaw's Song

O me, O me, what frugal cheer
My love doth feed upon!
A touch, a ray, that is not here,
A shadow that is gone:

A dream of breath that might be near,
An inly-echoed tone,
The thought that one may think me dear,
The place where one was known,

The tremor of a banished fear,
All, all that was not done –
O me, O me, what frugal cheer
My love doth feed upon!

George Eliot

From Dipsychus (Scene V)

O Rosalie, my precious maid,
I think thou thinkest love is true;
And on thy fragrant bosom laid
I almost could believe it too.

O in our nook, unknown, unseen,
We'll hold our fancy like a screen,
Us and the dreadful fact between,
And it shall yet be long, aye, long,
The quiet notes of our low song
Shall keep us from that sad dong, dong.
Hark, hark, hark! O voice of fear!
It reaches us here, even here!
Dong, there is no God; dong!

Ring ding, ring ding, tara, tara,
To battle, to battle – haste, haste –
To battle, to battle – aha, aha!
On, on, to the conqueror's feast.
From east and west, and south and north,
Ye men of valour and of worth,
Ye mighty men of arms, come forth,
And work your will, for that is just;
And in your impulse put your trust,
Beneath your feet the fools are dust.
Alas, alas! O grief and wrong,
The good are weak, the wicked strong;
And O my God, how long, how long?
Dong, there is no God; dong!

Ring, ting; to bow before the strong,
There is a rapture too in this;
Speak, outraged maiden, in thy wrong
Did terror bring no secret bliss?
Were boys' shy lips worth half a song
Compared to the hot soldier's kiss?

O Rosalie, my lovely maid,
I think thou thinkest love is true;
And on thy faithful bosom laid
I almost could believe it too.
The villainies, the wrongs, the alarms
Forget we in each other's arms.

No justice here, no God above;
But where we are, is there not love?
What? what? thou also go'st? For how
Should dead truth live in lover's vow?
What, thou? thou also lost? Dong
Dong, there is no God: dong!

Arthur Hugh Clough

'O! That 'Twere Possible'

Oh! That 'Twere Possible
After long grief and pain
To find the arms of my true-love
Round me once again! . . .

When I was wont to meet her
In the silent woody places
Of the land that gave me birth,
We stood tranced in long embraces,
Mixt with kisses sweeter, sweeter
Than any thing on earth

A shadow flits before me –
Not thou, but like to thee,
Ah God! that it were possible
For one short hour to see
The souls we loved, that they might tell us
What and where they be . . . !

Alfred, Lord Tennyson

Beeny Cliff

O the opal and the sapphire of that wandering western
    sea,
And the woman riding high above with bright hair
    flapping free –
The woman whom I loved so, and who loyally loved
    me.

The pale mews plained below us, and the waves seemed
    far away
In a nether sky, engrossed in saying their ceaseless
    babbling say,
As we laughed light-heartedly aloft on that clear-
    sunned March day.

A little cloud then cloaked us, and there flew an irised
    rain,
And the Atlantic dyed its levels with a dull misfeatured
    stain,
And then the sun burst out again, and purples prinked
    the main.

– Still in all its chasmal beauty bulks old Beeny to the
    sky,
And shall she and I not go there once again now March
    is nigh,
And the sweet things said in that March say anew there
    by and by?

What if still in chasmal beauty looms that wild weird
    western shore,
The woman now is – elsewhere – whom the ambling
    pony bore,
And nor knows nor cares for Beeny, and will laugh
    there nevermore.

Thomas Hardy

Body's Beauty
(From The House Of Life, Sonnet LXXVIII)

Of Adam's first wife, Lilith, it is told
(The witch he loved before the gift of Eve,)
That, ere the snake's, her sweet tongue could deceive,
And her enchanted hair was the first gold.
And still she sits, young while the earth is old,
And, subtly of herself contemplative,
Draws men to watch the bright web she can weave,
Till heart and body and life are in its hold.

The rose and poppy are her flowers; for where
Is he not found, O Lilith, whom shed scent
And soft-shed kisses and soft sleep shall snare?
Lo! as that youth's eyes burned at thine, so went
Thy spell through him, and left his straight neck bent
And round his heart one strangling golden hair.

Dante Gabriel Rossetti

Chamber Music XXII

Of that so sweet imprisonment
My soul, dearest, is fain –
Soft arms that woo me to relent
And woo me to detain.
Ah, could they ever hold me there,
Gladly were I a prisoner!

Dearest, through interwoven arms
By love made tremulous,
That night allures me where alarms
Nowise may trouble us
But sleep to dreamier sleep be wed
Where soul with soul lies prisoned.

James Joyce

Appeal

Oh, I am very weary,
Though tears no longer flow;
My eyes are tired of weeping,
My heart is sick of woe.

My life is very lonely,
My days pass heavily,
I'm weary of repining,
Wilt thou not come to me?

Oh didst thou know my longings
For thee, from day to day,
My hopes, so often blighted,
Thou wouldst not thus delay!

Anne Brontë

Dead Love

Oh never weep for love that's dead
Since love is seldom true
But changes his fashion from blue to red,
From brightest red to blue,
And love was born to an early death
And is so seldom true.

Then harbour no smile on your bonny face
To win the deepest sigh.
The fairest words on truest lips
Pass on and surely die,
And you will stand alone, my dear,
When wintry winds draw nigh.

Sweet, never weep for what cannot be,
For this God has not given.
If the merest dream of love were true
Then, sweet, we should be in heaven,
And this is only earth, my dear,
Where true love is not given.

Elizabeth Siddal

To The Beloved

Oh, not more subtly silence strays
Amongst the winds, between the voices,
Mingling alike with pensive lays,
And with the music that rejoices,
Than thou art present in my days.

My silence, life returns to thee
In all the pauses of her breath,
Hush back to rest the melody
That out of thee awakeneth;
And thou, wake ever, wake for me!

Thou art like silence all unvexed,
Though wild words part my soul from thee,
Thou art like silence unperplexed,
A secret and a mystery
Between one footfall and the next.

Most dear pause in a mellow lay!
Thou art inwoven with every air.
With thou the wildest tempests play,
And snatches of thee everywhere
Make little heavens throughout a day.

Darkness and solitude shine, for me.
For life's fair outward part are rife
The silver noises; let them be.
It is the very soul of life
Listens for thee, listens for thee.

O pause between the sobs of cares;
O thought within all thought that is;
Trance between laughters unawares:
Thou art the shape of melodies,
And thou the ecstasy of prayers!

Alice Meynell

The River

On the broad-bosomed lordly Thames
Down which we glide, the August sun
In mellow evening splendour flames;
Soon will our voyage all be done.

Wrapped in thy shawl, in still repose
Back in the stern-seat soft-reclined,
Round thy sweet form the cool air blows,
And thy veil flutters in the wind.

While I, crouched further yet astern,
Wait for the voice that flowed erewhile,
Wait for the graceful head to turn,
And lightly look, and gaily smile.

But ah, the head keeps turned away;
I only see those fingers small
Flit charmingly in careless play
Through the green fringes of thy shawl.

Ah, let the harmless fringes float,
Let the shawl be; for it leaves bare
A lovely strip of thy soft throat
Gleaming between it and thy hair.

And see – for sleep his heavy balms
On all our tired crew outpours –
With half-shut eyes and languid arms
The rowers dip and lift their oars.

Still glides the stream, slow drops the boat
Under the rustling poplars' shade;
Silent the swans beside us float –
None speaks, none heeds; ah, turn thy head!

Let those arch eyes now softly shine,
That mocking mouth grow sweetly bland;
Ah, let them rest, those eyes, on mine!
On mine let rest that lovely hand!

My pent-up tears oppress my brain,
My heart is swollen with love unsaid.
Ah, let me weep, and tell my pain,
And on thy shoulder rest my head!

Before I die – before the soul,
Which now is mine, must re-attain
Immunity from my control,
And wander round the world again;

Before this teased o'erlaboured heart
For ever leaves its vain employ,
Dead to its deep habitual smart,
And dead to hopes of future joy.

Matthew Arnold

Dreaming

Once, in a dream-hour's ghostly glimmering light,
One set her face for her love's dwelling-place;
With flying feet, and heart that beat apace,
The wan dream-soul went out into the night;
Adown pale paths she passed in breathless flight
Nor noted how the dear, familiar ways
Were stranger grown in this sad, strange moon's rays:
Lo! and at last her love's home came in sight.

Yea, at his door she knocked and cried till morn.
And moaned around his house, and knocked again,
Calling on love's dear name; but love was dead.
Empty was all, and desolate, and forlorn,
Lost like her heart; and still the weary rain,
And the wind's voices wailing overhead.

Katharine Tynan

Once We Played

Once we played at love together –
Played it smartly, if you please;
Lightly, as a windblown feather,
Did we stake a heart apiece.

Oh, it was delicious fooling!
In the hottest of the game,
Without thought of future cooling,
All too quickly burned life's flame.

In this give-and-take of glances,
Kisses sweet as honey dews,
When we played with equal chances,
Did you win, or did I lose?

Mathilde Blind

A Face From The Past

Out of the Past there has come a Face;
Wherefore I do not know;
I did not call it from its place,
I cannot make it go;
In the night it was very near,
And it looks at me to-day,
With well-known eyes, so kind, so dear,
And it will not go away.

I am the same that I was before,
There is nothing new to say;
But *this* is with me evermore,
As it was not yesterday;
It makes the Moment vague and vain,
And (what a wondrous thing!)
I hear an old tale told again
As if it was happening.

You talk, but scarce I understand;
If you but pause for breath,
Straightway I am in that far land
Beyond the seas of Death;
All living sights are dimly seen
Across that mighty space –
How can I tell you what I mean?
'Tis nothing but a Face.

O friends, who think me dull or cold,
Why do you feel surprise?
Have *you* no memories that hold
Your weary waking eyes?
I want to take all patiently,
But I sometimes long to say,
A Face has come from the Past to me –
Let me alone to-day!

Menella Bute Smedley

Now

Out of your whole life give but a moment!
All of your life that has gone before,
All to come after it, – so you ignore,
So you make perfect the present, – condense,
In a rapture of rage, for perfection's endowment,
Thought and feeling and soul and sense –
Merged in a moment which gives me at last
You around me for once, you beneath me, above me –
Me – sure that despite of time future, time past, –
This tick of our life-time's one moment you love me!
How long such suspension may linger? Ah, sweet –
The moment eternal – just that and no more –
When ecstasy's utmost we clutch at the core
While cheeks burn, arms open, eyes shut and lips meet!

Robert Browning

The Lover Mourns For the Loss Of Love

Pale brows, still hands and dim hair,
I had a beautiful friend
And dreamed that the old despair
Would end in love in the end:
She looked in my heart one day
And saw your image was there;
She has gone weeping away.

W. B. Yeats

To —— , To Powder Her Neck

Powder your neck lest these be seen
The marks where kissing lips have been.
But have a care the powder be
Matched to your round neck's ivorie
Lest by the difference of hue
Suspicion fall on me and you.

Oliver St John Gogarty

Cean Dubh Deelish
(Translation of an Irish Song)

Put your head, darling, darling, darling,
Your darling black head my heart above;
Oh, mouth of honey, with the thyme for fragrance,
Who, with heart in breast, could deny you love?
Oh, many and many a young girl for me is pining,
Letting her locks of gold to the cold wind free,
For me, the foremost of our gay young fellows;
But I'd leave a hundred, pure love, for thee!
Then put your head, darling, darling, darling,
Your darling black head my heart above;
Oh, mouth of honey, with the thyme for fragrance,
Who, with heart in breast, could deny you love?

Sir Samuel Ferguson

She Weeps Over Rahoon

Rain on Rahoon falls softly, softly falling,
Where my dark lover lies.
Sad is his voice that calls me, sadly calling,
At grey moonrise.

Love, hear thou
How soft, how sad his voice is ever calling,
Ever unanswered, and the dark rain falling,
Then as now.

Dark too our hearts, O love, shall lie and cold
As his sad heart has lain
Under the moongrey nettles, the black mould
And muttering rain.

James Joyce

Remember

Remember me when I am gone away,
Gone far away into the silent land;
When you can no more hold me by the hand,
Nor I half turn to go, yet turning stay.
Remember me when no more day by day
You tell me of our future that you planned:
Only remember me; you understand
It will be late to counsel then or pray.
Yet if you should forget me for a while
And afterwards remember, do not grieve:
For if the darkness and corruption leave
A vestige of the thoughts that once I had,
Better by far you should forget and smile
Than that you should remember and be sad.

Christina Rossetti

Ringleted Youth Of My Love

(From the Irish)

Ringleted youth of my love,
With thy locks bound loosely behind thee,
You passed by the road above,
But you never came in to find me;
Where were the harm for you
If you came for a little to see me,
Your kiss is a wakening dew
Were I ever so ill or so dreamy.

If I had golden store
I would make a nice little boreen
To lead straight up to his door,
The door of the house of my storeen;
Hoping to God not to miss
The sound of his footfall in it,
I have waited so long for his kiss
That for days I have slept not a minute.

I thought, O my love! you were so –
As the moon is, or sun on a fountain,
And I thought after that you were snow,
The cold snow on top of the mountain;
And I thought after that, you were more
Like God's lamp shining to find me,
Or the bright star of knowledge before,
And the star of knowledge behind me.

You promised me high-heeled shoes,
And satin and silk, my storeen,
And to follow me, never to lose,
Though the ocean were round us roaring;
Like a bush in a gap in a wall
I am now left lonely without thee,
And this house I grow dead of, is all
That I see around or about me.

Douglas Hyde

Song

Say what is love – to live in vain
To live and die and live again

Say what is love – is it to be
In prison still and still be free.

Or seems as free – alone and prove
The hopeless hopes of real love?

Does real love on earth exist?
'Tis like a sunbeam on the mist

That fades and nowhere will remain
And nowhere is o'ertook again.

Say what is love – a blooming name
A rose leaf on the page of fame

That blooms then fades – to cheat no more
And is what nothing was before.

Say what is love – what e'er it be
It centres, Mary, still with thee.

John Clare

School Parted Us
(From Brother And Sister, Sonnet XI)

School parted us; we never found again
That childish world where our two spirits mingled
Like scents from varying roses that remain
One sweetness, nor can evermore be singled.

Yet the twin habit of that early time
Lingered for long about the heart and tongue:
We had been natives of one happy clime
And its dear accent to our utterance clung.

Till the dire years whose awful name is Change
Had grasped our souls still yearning in divorce,
And pitiless shaped them in two forms that range
Two elements which sever their life's course.

But were another childhood-world my share,
I would be born a little sister there.

George Eliot

Queens

Seven dog-days we let pass
Naming Queens in Glenmacnass,
All the rare and royal names
Wormy sheepskin yet retains,
Etain, Helen, Maeve, and Fand,
Golden Deirdre's tender hand,
Bert, the big-foot, sung by Villon,
Cassandra, Ronsard found in Lyon.
Queens of Sheba, Meath and Connaught,
Coifed with crown, or gaudy bonnet,
Queens whose finger once did stir men,
Queens were eaten of fleas and vermin,
Queens men drew like Monna Lisa,
Or slew with drugs in Rome and Pisa,
We named Lucrezia Crivelli,
And Titian's lady with amber belly,
Queens acquainted in learned sin,
Jane of Jewry's slender shin:
Queens who cut the bogs of Glanna,

Judith of Scripture, and Gloriana,
Queens who wasted the East by proxy,
Or drove the ass-cart, a tinker's doxy,
Yet these are rotten – I ask their pardon –
And we've the sun on rock and garden,
These are rotten, so you're the Queen
Of all are living, or have been.

J. M. Synge

A Quoi Bon Dire

Seventeen years ago you said
Something that sounded like Good-bye;
And everybody thinks that you are dead,
But I.

So I, as I grow stiff and cold
To this and that say Good-bye too;
And everybody sees that I am old
But you.

And one fine morning in a sunny lane
Some boy and girl will meet and kiss and swear
That nobody can love their way again
While over there
You will have smiled, I shall have tossed your hair.

Charlotte Mew

She Charged Me

She charged me with having said this and that
To another woman long years before,
In the very parlour where we sat, –

Sat on a night when the endless pour
Of rain on the roof and the road below
Bent the spring of the spirit more and more . . .

– So charged she me: and the Cupid's bow
Of her mouth was hard, and her eyes, and her face,
And her white forefinger lifted slow.

Had she done it gently, or shown a trace
That not too curiously would she view
A folly flown ere her reign had place,

A kiss might have closed it. But, I knew
From the fall of each word, and the pause between,
That the curtain would drop upon us two
Ere long, in our play of slave and queen.

Thomas Hardy

The End Of It

She did not love to love, but hated him
For making her to love; and so her whim
From passion taught misprision to begin.
And all this sin
Was because love to cast out had no skill
Self, which was regent still.
Her own self-will made void her own self's will.

Francis Thompson

Ruth

She stood breast-high amid the corn,
Clasped by the golden light of morn,
Like the sweetheart of the sun,
Who many a glowing kiss had won.

On her cheek an autumn flush,
Deeply ripened; – such a blush
In the midst of brown was born,
Like red poppies grown with corn.

Round her eyes her tresses fell,
Which were blackest none could tell,
But long lashes veiled a light,
That had else been all too bright.

And her hat, with shady brim,
Made her tressy forehead dim;
Thus she stood amid the stooks,
Praising God with sweetest looks: –

Sure, I said, Heaven did not mean,
Where I reap thou shouldst but glean,
Lay thy sheaf adown and come,
Share my harvest and my home.

Thomas Hood

A Girl At Her Devotions

She was just risen from her bended knee,
But yet peace seemed not with her piety;
For there was paleness upon her young cheek,
And thoughts upon the lips which never speak,
But wring the heart that at the last they break,

Alas! how much of misery may be read
In that wan forehead, and that bowed down head: –
Her eye is on a picture, woe that ever
Love should thus struggle with a vain endeavour
Against itself: it is a common tale,
And ever will be while earth soils prevail
Over earth's happiness; it tells she strove
With silent, secret, unrequited love.

It matters not its history; love has wings
Like lightning, swift and fatal, and it springs
Like a wild flower where it is least expected,
Existing whether cherished or rejected;
Living with only but to be content,
Hopeless, for love is its own element, –
Requiring nothing so that it may be
The martyr of its fond fidelity.
A mystery art thou, thou mighty one!
We speak thy name in beauty, yet we shun
To own thee, Love, a guest; the poet's songs
Are sweetest when their voice to thee belongs,
And hope, sweet opiate, tenderness, delight,
Are terms which are thy own peculiar right;
Yet all deny their master, – who will own
His breast thy footstool, and his heart thy throne?

– 'Tis strange to think if we could fling aside
The masque and mantle that love wears from pride,
How much would be, we now so little guess,
Deep in each heart's undreamed, unsought recess.
The careless smile, like a gay banner borne,
The laught of merriment, the lip of scorn, –
And for a cloak what is there that can be
So difficult to pierce as gaiety?
Too dazzling to be scanned, the haughty brow
Seems to hide something it would not avow;
But rainbow words, light laugh, and thoughtless jest,
These are the bars, the curtain to the breast,

That shuns a scrutiny: and she, whose form
Now bends in grief beneath the bosom's storm,
Has hidden well her wound, – now none are nigh
To mock with curious or with careless eye,
(For love seeks sympathy, a chilling yes,
Strikes at the root of its best happiness,
And mockery is worm-wood), she may dwell
On feelings which that picture may not tell.

L. E. L.

Black Marble

Sick of pale European beauties spoiled
By false religions, all the cant of priests
And mimic virtues, far away I toiled
In lawless lands, with savage men and beasts.
Across the bloom-hung forest, in the way
Widened by lions or where the winding snake
Had pierced, I counted not each night and day,
Till, gazing through a flower-encumbered brake,
I crouched down like a panther watching prey –
Black Venus stood beside a sultry lake.

The naked negress raised on high her arms,
Round as palm-saplings; cup-shaped either breast,
Unchecked by needless shames or cold alarms,
Swelled, like a burning mountain, with the zest
Of inward life, and tipped itself with fire:
Fashioned to crush a lover of a foe,
Her proud limbs owned their strength, her waist its
    span,

Her fearless form its faultless curves. And lo! –
The lion and the serpent and the man
Watched her the while with each his own desire.

Arthur O'Shaughnessy

To a Woman

Since all that I can do for thee
Is to do nothing, this my prayer must be;
That thou may'st never guess nor ever see
The all-endured this nothing-done costs me.

Owen Meredith, Lord Lytton

The Lover's Farewell

Slowly through the tomb-still streets I go –
Morn is dark, save one swart streak of gold –
Sullen rolls the far-off river's flow,
And the moon is very thin and cold.

Long and long before the house I stand
Where sleeps she, the dear, dear one I love –
All undreaming that I leave my land,
Mute and mourning, like the moon above!

Wishfully I stretch abroad mine arms
Towards the well-remembered casement-cell –
Fare thee well! Farewell thy virgin charms!
And thou stilly, stilly house, farewell!

And farewell the dear dusk little room,
Redolent of roses as a dell,

And the lattice that relieved its gloom –
And its pictured lilac walls, farewell!

Forth upon my path! I must not wait –
Bitter blows the fretful morning wind:
Warden, wilt thou softly close the gate
When thou knowest I leave my heart behind?

James Clarence Mangan

The Charming Woman

So Miss Myrtle is going to marry?
What a number of hearts she will break!
There's Lord George, and Tom Brown, and Sir Harry,
Who are dying of love for her sake!
'Tis a match that we all must approve, –
Let gossips say all that they can!
For indeed she's a charming woman,
And he's a most fortunate man!

Yes, indeed, she's a charming woman,
And she reads both Latin and Greek, –
And I'm told that she solved a problem
In Euclid before she could speak!
Had she been but a daughter of mine,
I'd have taught her to hem and to sew, –
But her mother (a charming woman)
Couldn't think of such trifles, you know!

Oh, she's really a charming woman!
But, perhaps, a little too thin;
And no wonder such very late hours
Should ruin her beautiful skin!
And her shoulders are rather too bare,
And her gown's nearly up to her knees,

But I'm told that these charming women
May dress themselves just as they please!

Yes, she's really a charming woman!
But, I thought, I observed, by the bye,
A something – that's rather uncommon, –
In the flash of that very bright eye?
It may be a mere fancy of mine,
Though her voice has a very sharp tone, –
But I'm told that these charming women
Are inclined to have wills of their own!

She sings like a bullfinch or linnet,
And she talks like an Archbishop too;
Can play you a rubber and win it, –
If she's got nothing better to do!
She can chatter of Poor-laws and Tithes,
And the value of labour and land, –
'Tis a pity when charming women
Talk of things which they don't understand!

I'm told that she hasn't a penny,
Yet her gowns would make Maradan stare;
And I feel her bills must be many, –
But that's only her husband's affair!
Such husbands are very uncommon,
So regardless of prudence and pelf, –
But they say such a charming woman
Is a fortune, you know, in herself!

She's brothers and sisters by dozens,
And all charming people, they say!
And several tall Irish cousins,
Whom she loves in a sisterly way.
O young men, if you'd take my advice,
You would find it an excellent plan, –
Don't marry a charming woman,
If you are a sensible man!

Helen Selina, Lady Dufferin

Abroad

Some go to game, or pray in Rome
I travel for my turning home
For when I've been six months abroad
Faith your kiss would brighten God!

J. M. Synge

Love's Trinity

Soul, heart, and body we thus singly name,
Are not in love divisible and distinct,
But each with each inseparably linked.
One is not honour, and the other shame,
But burn as closely fused as fuel, heat, and flame.

They do not love who give the body and keep
The heart ungiven; nor they who yield the soul, –
And guard the body. Love doth give the whole;
Its range being high as heaven, as ocean deep,
Wide as the realms of air or planet's curving sweep.

Alfred Austin

After Long Silence

Speech after long silence; it is right,
All other lovers being estranged or dead,
Unfriendly lamplight hid under its shade,
The curtains drawn upon unfriendly night,
That we descant and yet again descant
Upon the supreme theme of Art and Song:
Bodily decrepitude is wisdom; young
We loved each other and were ignorant.

W. B. Yeats

The Look

Strephon kissed me in the spring,
Robin in the fall,
But Colin only looked at me
And never kissed at all.

Strephon's kiss was lost in jest,
Robin's lost in play,
But the kiss in Colin's eyes
Haunts me night and day.

Sara Teasdale

The Terrace At Berne

Ten years! and to my waking eye
Once more the roofs of Berne appear;
The rocky banks, the terrace high,
The stream! – and do I linger here?

The clouds are on the Oberland,
The Jungfrau snows look faint and far;
But bright are those green fields at hand,
And through those fields comes down the Aar,

And from the blue twin-lakes it comes,
Flows by the town, the churchyard fair;
And 'neath the garden-walk it hums,
The house! – and is my Marguerite there?

Ah, shall I see thee, while a flush
Of startled pleasure floods thy brow,
Quick through the oleanders brush,
And clap thy hands, and cry: '*Tis thou!*

Or hast thou long since wandered back,
Daughter of France! to France, thy home;
And flitted down the flowery track
Where feet like thine too lightly come?

Doth riotous laughter now replace
Thy smile; and rouge, with stony glare,
Thy cheek's soft hue; and fluttering lace
The kerchief that enwound thy hair?

Or is it over! – art thou dead?
Dead! – and no warning shiver ran
Across my heart, to say thy thread
Of life was cut, and closed thy span!

Could from earth's ways that figure slight
Be lost, and I not feel 'twas so?
Of that fresh voice the gay delight
Fail from earth's air, and I not know?

Or shall I find thee still, but changed,
But not the Marguerite of thy prime?
With all thy being re-arranged,
Passed through the crucible of time;

With spirit vanished, beauty waned,
And hardly yet a glance, a tone,
A gesture – anything – retained
Of all that was my Marguerite's own?

I will not know! For wherefore try,
To things by mortal course that live,
A shadow durability,
For which they were not meant, to give?

Like driftwood spars, which meet and pass
Upon the boundless ocean-plain,
So on the sea of life, alas!
Man meets man – meets, and quits again.

I knew it when my life was young;
I feel it still, now youth is o'er.
– The mists are on the mountain hung,
And Marguerite I shall see no more.

Matthew Arnold

The Marriage Vow

The altar, 'tis of death! for there are laid
The sacrifice of all youth's sweetest hopes.
It is a dreadful thing for woman's lip
To swear the heart away; yet know that heart
Annuls the vow while speaking, and shrinks back
From the dark future that it dares not face.
The service read above the open grave
Is far less terrible than that which seals
The vow that binds the victim, not the will:
For in the grave is rest.

L. E. L.

Endymion

(For music)

The apple trees are hung with gold,
And birds are loud in Arcady,
The sheep lie bleating in the fold,
The wild goat runs across the wold,
But yesterday his love he told,
I know he will come back to me.
O rising moon! O Lady moon!
Be you my lover's sentinel,
You cannot choose but know him well.
For he is shod with purple shoon,
You cannot choose but know my love,
For he a shepherd's crook doth bear,
And he is soft as any dove,
And brown and curly is his hair.

The turtle now has ceased to call
Upon her crimson-footed groom,
The grey wolf prowls about the stall,
The lily's singing seneschal
Sleeps in the lily-bell, and all
The violet hills are lost in gloom.
O risen moon! O holy moon!
Stand on the top of Helice,
And if my own true love you see,
Ah! if you see the purple shoon,
The hazel crook, the lad's brown hair,
The goat-skin wrapped about his arm,
Tell him that I am waiting where
The rushlight glimmers in the Farm.

The falling dew is cold and chill,
And no bird sings in Arcady,
The little fauns have left the hill,
Even the tired daffodil
Has closed its gilded doors, and still

My lover comes not back to me.
False moon! False moon! O waning moon!
Where is my own true lover gone,
Where are the lips vermilion,
The shepherd's crook, the purple shoon?
Why spread that silver pavilion,
Why wear that veil of drifting mist?
Ah! thou hast young Endymion,
Thou hast the lips that should be kissed!

Oscar Wilde

The Blessed Damozel

The blessed damozel leaned out
From the gold bar of Heaven;
Her eyes were deeper than the depth
Of waters stilled at even;
She had three lilies in her hand,
And the stars in her hair were seven.

Her robe, ungirt from clasp to hem,
No wrought flowers did adorn,
But a white rose of Mary's gift,
For service meetly worn;
Her hair that lay along her back
Was yellow like ripe corn.

Herseemed she scarce had been a day
One of God's choristers;
The wonder was not yet quite gone
From that still look of hers;
Albeit, to them she left, her day
Had counted as ten years.

(To one, it is ten years of years.
. . . Yet now, and in this place,
Surely she leaned o'er me – her hair
Fell all about my face. . . .
Nothing: the autumn-fall of leaves.
The whole year sets apace.)

It was the rampart of God's house
That she was standing on;
By God built over the sheer depth
The which is Space begun;
So high, that looking downward thence
She scarce could see the sun.

It lies in Heaven, across the flood
Of ether, as a bridge.
Beneath, the tides of day and night
With flame and darkness ridge
The void, as low as where this earth
Spins like a fretful midge.

Around her, lovers, newly met
'Mid deathless love's acclaims,
Spoke evermore among themselves
Their heart-remembered names;
And the souls mounting up to God
Went by her like thin flames.

And still she bowed herself and stooped
Out of the circling charm;
Until her bosom must have made
The bar she leaned on warm,
And the lilies lay as if asleep
Along her bended arm.

From the fixed place of Heaven she saw
Time like a pulse shake fierce
Through all the worlds. Her gaze still strove

Within the gulf to pierce
Its path; and now she spoke as when
The stars sang in their spheres

The sun was gone now; the curled moon
Was like a little feather
Fluttering far down the gulf, and now
She spoke through the still weather.
Her voice was like the voice the stars
Had when they sang together.

(Ah sweet! Even now, in that bird's song,
Strove not her accents there,
Fain to be hearkened? When those bells
Possessed the mid-day air,
Strove not her steps to reach my side
Down all the echoing stair?)

'I wish that he were come to me,
For he will come,' she said.
'Have I not prayed in Heaven? – on earth,
Lord, Lord, has he not prayed?
And not two prayers a perfect strength?
And shall I feel afraid?

'When round his head the aureole clings,
And he is clothed in white,
I'll take his hand and go with him
To the deep wells of light;
As unto a stream we will step down,
And bathe there in God's sight.

'We two will stand beside that shrine,
Occult, withheld, untrod,
Whose lamps are stirred continually
With prayer sent up to God;
And see our old prayers, granted, melt
Each like a little cloud.

'We two will lie i' the shadow of
That living mystic tree
Within whose secret growth the Dove
Is sometimes felt to be,
While every leaf that His plumes touch
Saith His Name audibly.

'And I myself will teach to him
I myself, lying so,
The songs I sing here; which his voice
Shall pause in, hushed and slow,
And find some knowledge at each pause,
Or some new thing to know.'

(Alas! we two, we two, thou say'st!
Yea, one wast thou with me
That once of old. But shall God lift
To endless unity
The soul whose likeness with thy soul
Was but its love for thee?'

'We two,' she said, 'will seek the groves
Where the lady Mary is,
With her five handmaidens, whose names
Are five sweet symphonies,
Cecily, Gertrude, Magdalen,
Margaret and Rosalys.

'Circlewise sit they, with bound locks
And foreheads garlanded;
Into the fine cloth white like flame
Weaving the golden thread,
To fashion the birth-robes for them
Who are just born, being dead.

'He shall fear, haply, and be dumb
Then will I lay my cheek
To his, and tell about our love,

Not once abashed or weak:
And the dear Mother will approve
My pride, and let me speak.

'Herself shall bring us, hand in hand,
To Him round whom all souls
Kneel, the clear-ranged unnumbered heads
Bowed with their aureoles:
And angels meeting us shall sing
To their citherns and citoles.

'There will I ask of Christ the Lord
Thus much for him and me: –
Only to live as once on earth
With Love, – only to be,
As then awhile, for ever now
Together, I and he.'

She gazed and listened and then said,
Less sad of speech than mild, –
'All this is when he comes.' She ceased.
The light thrilled towards her, filled
With angels in strong level flight.
Her eyes prayed, and she smiled.

(I saw her smile.) But soon their path
Was vague in distant spheres:
And then she cast her arms along
The golden barriers,
And laid her face between her hands,
And wept. (I heard her tears.)

Dante Gabriel Rossetti

From Two In The Campagna

The champaign with its endless fleece
Of feathery grasses everywhere!
Silence and passion, joy and peace,
An everlasting wash of air –
Rome's ghost since her decease.

Such life here, through such lengths of hours,
Such miracles performed in play,
Such primal naked forms of flowers,
Such letting nature have her way
While heaven looks from its towers!

How say you? Let us, O my dove,
Let us be unashamed of soul,
As earth lies bare to heaven above!
How is it under our control
To love or not to love?

I would that you were all to me,
You that are just so much, no more.
Nor yours nor mine, nor slave nor free!
Where does the fault lie? What the core
O' the wound, since wound must be?

I would I could adopt your will,
See with your eyes, and set my heart
Beating by yours, and drink my fill
At your soul's springs, – your part my part
In life, for good and ill.

No. I yearn upward, touch you close,
Then stand away. I kiss your cheek,
Catch your soul's warmth, – I pluck the rose
And love it more than tongue can speak –
Then the good minute goes.

Already how am I so far
Out of that minute? Must I go
Still like the thistle-ball, no bar,
Onward, whenever light winds blow,
Fixed by no friendly star?

Just when I seemed about to learn!
Where is the thread now? Off again!
The old trick! Only I discern –
Infinite passion, and the pain
Of finite hearts that yearn.

Robert Browning

Thee, Thee, Only Thee

The dawning of morn, the daylight's sinking,
The night's long hours still find me thinking
Of thee, thee, only thee.
When friends are met, and goblets crowned,
And smiles are near that once enchanted,
Unreached by all that sunshine round,
My soul, like some dark spot, is haunted
By thee, thee, only thee.

Whatever in fame's high path could waken
My spirit once is now forsaken
For thee, thee, only thee.
Like shores by which some headlong bark
To the ocean hurries, resting never,
Life's scenes go by me, bright or dark
I know not, heed not, hastening ever
To thee, thee, only thee.

I have not a joy but of thy bringing,
And pain itself seems sweet when springing

From thee, thee, only thee.
Like spells that nought on earth can break,
Till lips that know the charm have spoken,
This heart, howe'er the world may wake
Its grief, its scorn, can but be broken
By thee, thee, only thee.

Thomas Moore

The Evening Darkens Over

The evening darkens over
After a day so bright
The windcast waves discover
That wild will be the night.
There's sound of distant thunder

The latest sea-birds hover
Along the cliff's sheer height;
As in the memory wander
Last flutterings of delight,
White wings lost on the white.

There's not a ship in sight;
And as the sun goes under
Thick clouds conspire to cover
The moon that should rise yonder.
Thou art alone, fond lover.

Robert Bridges

The Girl I Love

The girl I love is comely, straight, and tall,
Down her white neck her auburn tresses fall.
Her dress is neat, her carriage light and free –
Here's a health to that charming maid, whoe'er she be!

The rose's blush but fades beside her cheek;
Her eyes are blue, her forehead pale and meek;
Her lips like cherries on a summer tree –
Here's a health to that charming maid, whoe'er she be!

When I go to the field no youth can lighter bound,
And I freely pay when the cheerful jug goes round;
The barrel is full, but its heart we soon shall see, –
Here's a health to that charming maid, whoe'er she be!

Had I the wealth that props the Saxon's reign,
Or the diamond crown that decks the King of Spain,
I'd yield them all if she kindly smiled on me, –
Here's a health to the maid I love, whoe'er she be!

Five pounds of gold for each lock of her hair I'd pay,
And five times five for my love one hour each day;
Her voice is more sweet than the thrush on its own
   green tree;
Then, my dear, may I drink a fond deep health to thee!

Jeremiah Joseph Callanan

Meeting At Night

The grey sea and the long black land;
And the yellow half-moon large and low;
And the startled little waves that leap
In fiery ringlets from their sleep,

As I gain the cove with pushing prow,
And quench its speed i' the slushy sand.

Then a mile of warm sea-scented beach;
Three fields to cross till a farm appears;
A tap at the pane, the quick sharp scratch
And blue spurt of a lighted match,
And a voice less loud through its joys and fears,
Than the two hearts beating each to each!

Robert Browning

The Hour Has Come to Part!
(From A Woman's Sonnets XII)

The hour has come to part! and it is best
The severing stroke should fall in one short day
Rather than fitful fever spoil my rest,
Watching each gradual sign of love's decay.
Go forth dear! thou hast much to do on earth;
In life's campaign there waits thee a great part –
Much to be won and conquered of more worth
Than this poor victory of a woman's heart –
For me, the light is dimmed, the dream has past –
I seek not gladness, yet may find content
Fulfilling each small duty, reach at last
Some goal of peace before my youth is spent.
But come whatever may, come weal or woe
I love thee, bless thee where so e'er thou go!

Augusta, Lady Gregory

Night and Hell And I

The mill-stream, now that noises cease,
Is all that does not hold its peace;
Under the bridge it murmurs by,
And here are night and hell and I.

Who made the world I cannot tell;
'Tis made, and here am I in hell.
My hand, though now my knuckles bleed,
I never soiled with such a deed.

And so, no doubt, in time gone by,
Some have suffered more than I,
Who only spend the night alone
And strike my fist upon the stone.

A. E. Housman

The Owl And The Pussy Cat

The Owl and the Pussy-Cat went to sea
In a beautiful pea-green boat.
They took some honey, and plenty of money
Wrapped up in a five-pound note.
The Owl looked up to the stars above,
And sang to a small guitar,
'O lovely Pussy! O Pussy, my love,
What a beautiful Pussy you are,
You are,
You are!
What a beautiful Pussy you are!'

Pussy said to the Owl, 'You elegant fowl!
How charmingly sweet you sing!
O let us be married! too long we have tarried:

But what shall we do for a ring?'
They sailed away, for a year and a day,
To the land where the Bong-Tree grows,
And there in a wood a Piggy-wig stood,
With a ring at the end of his nose,
His nose,
His nose!
With a ring at the end of his nose.

'Dear Pig, are you willing to sell for one shilling
Your ring?' Said the Piggy, 'I will.'
So they took it away, and were married next day
By the Turkey who lives on the hill.
They dined on mince, and slices of quince,
Which they ate with a runcible spoon;
And hand in hand, on the edge of the sand
They danced by the light of the moon,
The moon,
The moon,
They danced by the light of the moon.

Edward Lear

Porphyria's Lover

The rain set early in to-night,
The sullen wind was soon awake,
It tore the elm-tops down for spite,
And did its worst to vex the lake:
I listened with heart fit to break.
When glided in Porphyria; straight
She shut the cold out and the storm,
And kneeled and made the cheerless grate
Blaze up, and all the cottage warm;
Which done, she rose, and from her form
Withdrew the dripping cloak and shawl,

And laid her soiled gloves by, untied
Her hat and let the damp hair fall,
And, last, she sat down by my side
And called me. When no voice replied,
She put my arm about her waist,
And made her smooth white shoulder bare,
And all her yellow hair displaced,
And, stooping, made my cheek lie there,
And spread, o'er all, her yellow hair,
Murmuring how she loved me – she
Too weak, for all her heart's endeavour,
To set its struggling passion free
From pride, and vainer ties dissever,
And give herself to me for ever.
But passion sometimes would prevail,
Nor could to-night's gay feast restrain
A sudden thought of one so pale
For love of her, and all in vain:
So, she came through wind and rain.
Be sure I looked up at her eyes
Happy and proud; at last I knew
Porphyria worshipped me; surprise
Made my heart swell, and still it grew
While I debated what to do.
That moment she was mine, mine, fair,
Perfectly pure and good: I found
A thing to do, and all her hair
In one long yellow string I wound
Three times her little throat around,
And strangled her. No pain felt she;
I am quite sure she felt no pain.
As a shut bud that holds a bee,
I warily oped her lids: again
Laughed the blue eyes without a stain.
And I untightened next the tress
About her neck; her cheek once more
Blushed bright beneath my burning kiss:
I propped her head up as before,

Only, this time my shoulder bore
Her head, which droops upon it still:
The smiling rosy little head,
So glad it has its utmost will,
That all it scorned at once is fled,
And I, its love, am gained instead!
Porphyria's love: she guessed not how
Her darling one wish would be heard.
And thus we sit together now,
And all night long we have not stirred,
And yet God has not said a word!

Robert Browning

A White Rose

The red rose whispers of passion,
And the white rose breathes of love;
O, the red rose is a falcon,
And the white rose is a dove.

But I send you a cream-white rosebud
With a flush on its petal tips;
For the love that is purest and sweetest
Has a kiss of desire on the lips.

John Boyle O'Reilly

The Woods Are Still

The woods are still that were so gay at primrose-
    springing,
Through the dry woods the brown field-fares are
    winging,
And I alone of love, of love am singing.

I sing of love to the haggard palmer-worm,
Of love 'mid the crumpled oak-leaves that once were
   firm,
Laughing, I sing of love at the summer's term.

Of love, on a path where the snake's cast skin is lying,
Blue feathers on the floor, and no cuckoo flying;
I sing to the echo of my own voice crying.

Michael Field

Master And Guest

There came a man across the moor,
Fell and foul of face was he.
He left the path by the cross-roads three,
And stood in the shadow of the door.

I asked him in to bed and board.
I never hated any man so.
He said he could not say me No.
He sat in the seat of my own dear lord.

'Now sit you by my side!' he said,
'Else may I neither eat nor drink.
You would not have me starve, I think.'
He ate the offerings of the dead.

'I'll light you to your bed,' quoth I.
'My bed is yours – but light the way!'
I might not turn aside nor stay;
I showed him where we twain did lie.

The cock was trumpeting the morn.
He said: 'Sweet love, a long farewell!
You have kissed a citizen of Hell,
And a soul was doomed when you were born.

'Mourn, mourn no longer for your dear!
Him may you never meet above.
The gifts that Love hath given to Love,
Love gives away again to Fear.'

Mary E. Coleridge

To His Mistress

There comes an end to summer,
To spring showers and hoar rime;
His mumming to each mummer
Has somewhere end in time,
And since life ends and laughter,
And leaves fall and tears dry,
Who shall call love immortal,
When all that is must die?

Nay, sweet, let's leave unspoken
The vows the fates gainsay,
For all vows made are broken,
We love but while we may.
Let's kiss when kissing pleases,
And part when kisses pall,
Perchance, this time to-morrow,
We shall not love at all.

You ask my love completest,
As strong next year as now,
The devil take you, sweetest,
Ere I make aught such vow.
Life is a masque that changes,

A fig for constancy!
No love at all were better,
Than love which is not free.

Ernest Dowson

The Azalea

There, where the sun shines first
Against our room,
She trained the gold Azalea, whose perfume
She, Spring-like, from her breathing grace dispersed.
Last night the delicate crests of saffron bloom,
For this their dainty likeness watched and nurst,
Were just at point to burst.
At dawn I dreamed, O God, that she was dead,
And groaned aloud upon my wretched bed,
And waked, ah, God, and did not waken her,
But lay, with eyes still closed,
Perfectly blessed in the delicious sphere
By which I knew so well that she was near,
My heart to speechless thankfulness composed.
Till 'gan to stir
A dizzy somewhat in my troubled head –
It *was* the azalea's breath, and she *was* dead!
The warm night had the lingering buds disclosed,
And I had fallen asleep with to my breast
A chance-found letter pressed
In which she said,
'So, till to-morrow eve, my Own, adieu!
Parting's well-paid with soon again to meet,
Soon in your arms to feel so small and sweet,
Sweet to myself that am so sweet to you!'

Coventry Patmore

My Love

There's not a fibre in my trembling frame
That does not vibrate when thy step draws near,
There's not a pulse that throbs not when I hear
Thy voice, thy breathing, nay thy very name.
When thou art with me every sense seems dim,
And all I am, or know, or feel is thee;
My soul grows faint, my veins run liquid flame,
And my bewildered spirit seems to swim
In eddying whirls of passion, dizzily.
When thou art gone, there creeps into my heart
A cold and bitter consciousness of pain;
The light, the warmth of life with thee depart,
And I sit dreaming over and over again
Thy greeting clasp, thy parting look and tone;
And suddenly I wake – and I am alone.

Fanny Kemble

A Pause

They made the chamber sweet with flowers and leaves,
And the bed sweet with flowers on which I lay;
While my soul, love-bound, loitered on its way.
I did not hear the birds about the eaves,
Nor hear the reapers talk among the sheaves:
Only my soul kept watch from day to day,
My thirsty soul kept watch for one away: –
Perhaps he loves, I thought, remembers, grieves.
At length there came the step upon the stair,
Upon the lock the old familiar hand:
Then first my spirit seemed to scent the air
Of Paradise; then first the tardy sand
Of time ran golden; and I felt my hair
Put on a glory, and my soul expand.

Christina Rossetti

Ballad Of The Bird-Bride

(Eskimo)

They never come back, though I loved them well;
I watch the South in vain;
The snow-bound skies are blear and grey,
Waste and wide is the wild gull's way,
And she comes never again.

Years agone, on the flat white strand,
I won my sweet sea-girl:
Wrapped in my coat of the snow-white fur,
I watched the wild birds settle and stir,
The grey gulls gather and whirl.

One, the greatest of all the flock,
Perched on an ice-floe bare,
Called and cried as her heart were broke,
And straight they were changed, that fleet bird-folk,
To women young and fair.

Swift I sprang from my hiding-place
And held the fairest fast;
I held her fast, the sweet, strange thing:
Her comrades skirled, but they all took wing,
And smote me as they passed.

I bore her safe to my warm snow house;
Full sweetly there she smiled;
And yet, whenever the shrill winds blew,
She would beat her long white arms anew,
And her eyes glanced quick and wild.

But I took her to wife, and clothed her warm
With skins of the gleaming seal;
Her wandering glances sank to rest
When she held a babe to her fair, warm breast,
And she loved me dear and leal.

Together we tracked the fox and the seal,
And at her behest I swore
That bird and beast my bow might slay
For meat and for raiment, day by day,
But never a grey gull more.

A weariful watch I keep for aye
'Mid the snow and the changeless frost:
Woe is me for my broken bird,
Woe, woe's me for my bonny bird,
My bird and the love-time lost!

Have ye forgotten the old keen life?
The hut with the skin-strewn floor?
O winged white wife, and children three,
Is there no room left in your hearts for me,
Or our home on the low sea-shore?

Once the quarry was scarce and shy,
Sharp hunger gnawed us sore,
My spoken oath was clean forgot,
My bow twanged thrice with a swift, straight shot,
And slew me sea-gulls four.

The sun hung red on the sky's dull breast,
The snow was wet and red;
Her voice shrilled out in a woeful cry,
She beat her long white arms on high,
'The hour is here,' she said.

She beat her arms, and she cried full fain
As she swayed and wavered there.
'Fetch me the feathers, my children three,
Feathers and plumes for you and me,
Bonny grey wings to wear!'

They ran to her side, our children three,
With the plumage black and grey;
Then she bent her down and drew them near,
She laid the plumes on our children dear,
'Mid the snow and the salt sea-spray.

'Babes of mine, of the wild wind's kin,
Feather ye quick, not stay.
Oh, oho! but the wild winds blow!
Babes of mine, it is time to go:
Up, dear hearts, and away!'

And lo! the grey plumes covered them all,
Shoulder and breast and brow.
I felt the wind of their whirling flight:
Was it sea or sky? was it day or night?
It is always night-time now.

Dear, will you never relent, come back?
I loved you long and true.
O winged white wife, and our children three,
Of the wild wind's kin though ye surely be,
Are ye not of my kin too?

Ay, ye once were mine, and, till I forget,
Ye are mine forever and aye,
Mine, wherever your wild wings go,
While shrill winds whistle across the snow
And the skies are blear and grey.

Rosamund Marriott Watson

Those Who Love The Most

Those who love the most,
Do not talk of their love,
Francesca, Guinevere,
Deirdre, Iseult, Heloise,
In the fragrant gardens of heaven
Are silent, or speak if at all
Of fragile inconsequent things.

And a woman I used to know
Who loved one man from her youth,
Against the strength of the fates
Fighting in sombre pride
Never spoke of this thing,
But hearing his name by chance,
A light would pass over her face.

Sara Teasdale

Love Song

Though the wind shakes lintel and rafter,
And the priest sits mourning alone,
For the ruin that comes hereafter
When the world shall be overthrown,
What matter the wind and weather
To those that live for a day?
When my Love and I are together,
What matter what men may say?

I and my love where the wild red rose is,
When hands grow weary and eyes are bright,
Kisses are sweet as the evening closes,
Lips are reddest before the night,
And what matter if Death be an endless slumber

And thorns the commonest crown for the head,
What matter if sorrow like wild weeds cumber,
When kisses are sweetest, and lips are red?

I that am only the idlest singer
That ever sang by a desolate sea,
A goodlier gift than song can bring her,
Sweeter than sound of minstrelsy,
For singers grow weary, and lips will tire,
And winds will scatter the pipe and reed,
And even the sound of the silver lyre
Sickens my heart in the days of need,
But never at all do I fail or falter
For I know that Love is a god, and fair,
And if death and derision follow after,
The only god worth a sin and a prayer.

And She and I are as Queen and Master,
Why should we care if a people groan
Neath a despot's feet, or some red disaster
Shatter the fool on his barren throne?
What matter if prisons and palaces crumble,
And the red flag floats in the piled-up street,
When over the sound of the cannon's rumble
The voice of my Lady is clear and sweet?
For the worlds are many and we are single,
And sweeter to me when my Lady sings,
Than the cry when the East and the West world mingle,
For clamour of battle, and the fall of Kings.

So out of the reach of tears and sorrow
Under the wild-rose let us play,
And if death and severing come tomorrow,
I have your kisses, sweet heart, today.

Oscar Wilde

The Farmer's Bride

Three Summers since I chose a maid,
Too young maybe – but more's to do
At harvest-time than bide and woo.
When us was wed she turned afraid
Of love and me and all things human;
Like the shut of a winter's day.
Her smile went out, and 'twasn't a woman –
More like a little frightened fay.
One night, in the Fall, she runned away.

'Out 'mong the sheep, her be,' they said,
'Should properly have been abed;
But sure enough she wasn't there
Lying awake with her wide brown stare.
So over seven-acre field and up-along across the down
We chased her, flying like a hare
Before our lanterns. To Church-Town
All in a shiver and a scare
We caught her, fetched her home at last
And turned the key upon her, fast.

She does the work about the house
As well as most, but like a mouse:
Happy enough to chat and play
With birds and rabbits and such as they,
So long as men-folk keep away.
'Not near, not near!' her eyes beseech
When one of us comes within reach.
The women say that beasts in stall
Look round like children at her call.
I've hardly heard her speak at all.

Shy as a leveret, swift as he,
Straight and slight as a young larch tree,
Sweet as the first wild violets, she,
To her wild self. But what to me?

The short days shorten and the oaks are brown,
The blue smoke rises to the low grey sky,
One leaf in the still air falls slowly down,
A magpie's spotted feathers lie
On the black earth spread white with rime,
The berries redden up to Christmas-time.
What's Christmas-time without there be
Some other in the house than we!

She sleeps up in the attic there
Alone, poor maid. 'Tis but a stair
Betwixt us. Oh! my God! the down,
The soft young down of her, the brown,
The brown of her – her eyes, her hair, her hair!

Charlotte Mew

Modern Love L

Thus piteously Love closed what he begat:
The union of this ever-diverse pair!
These two were rapid falcons in a snare,
Condemned to do the flitting of the bat.
Lovers beneath the singing sky of May,
They wandered once; clear as the dew on flowers:
But they fed not on the advancing hours:
Their hearts held cravings for the buried day.
Then each applied to each that fatal knife,
Deep questioning, which probes to endless dole.
Ah, what a dusty answer gets the soul
When hot for certainties in this our life! –
In tragic hints here see what evermore
Moves dark as yonder midnight ocean's force,
Thundering like ramping hosts of warrior horse
To throw that faint thin line upon the shore!

George Meredith

The Chamois Hunter's Love

For all his wildness and proud phantasies,
I love him!
Croly

Thy heart is in the upper world, where fleet the chamois
    bounds,
Thy heart is where the mountain-fir shakes to the
    torrent-sounds;
And where the snow-peaks gleam like stars, through
    the stillness of the air,
And where the Lauwine's peal is heard – Hunter! thy
    heart is there!

I know thou lovest me well, dear friend! but better,
    better far,
Thou lovest that high and haughty life, with rocks and
    storms at war;
In the green sunny vales with me, thy spirit would but
    pine,
And yet I will be thine, my love! and yet I will be thine!

And I will not seek to woo thee down from those thy
    native heights,
With the sweet song, our land's own song, of pastoral
    delights;
For thou must live as eagles live, thy path is not as mine,
And yet I will be thine, my love! and yet I will be thine.

And I will leave my blessed home, my father's joyous
    hearth,
With all the voices meeting there in tenderness and
    mirth,
With all the kind and laughing eyes, that in its firelight
    shine,
To sit forsaken in thy hut, yet know that thou art mine!

It is my youth, it is my bloom, it is my glad free heart,
That I cast away for thee – for thee, all reckless as thou
   art!
With tremblings and with vigils lone, I bind myself to
   dwell,
Yet, yet I would not change that lot, oh no! I love too
   well!

A mournful thing is love which grows to one so wild as
   thou,
With that bright restlessness of eye, that tameless fire of
   brow!
Mournful! – but dearer far I call its mingled fear and
   pride,
And the trouble of its happiness, than aught on earth
   beside.

To listen for thy step in vain, to start at every breath,
To watch through long long nights of storm, to sleep
   and dream of death,
To wake in doubt and loneliness – this doom I know is
   mine,
And yet I will be thine, my love! and yet I will be thine!

That I may greet thee from thine Alps, when thence
   thou comest at last,
That I may hear thy thrilling voice tell o'er danger past,
That I may kneel and pray for thee, and win thee aid
   divine,
For this I will be thine, my love! for this I will be thine!

Felicia Hemans

Modern Love XXIII

'Tis Christmas weather, and a country house
Receives us: rooms are full: we can but get
An attic-crib. Such lovers will not fret
At that, it is half-said. The great carouse
Knocks hard upon the midnight's hollow door,
But when I knock at hers, I see the pit.
Why did I come here in that dullard fit?
I enter, and lie couched upon the floor.
Passing, I caught the coverlet's quick beat: –
Come, Shame, burn to my soul! and Pride, and Pain –
Foul demons that have tortured me, enchain!
Out in the freezing darkness the lambs bleat.
The small bird stiffens in the low starlight.
I know not how, but shuddering as I slept,
I dreamed a banished angel to me crept:
My feet were nourished on her breasts all night.

George Meredith

'Tis Well To Wake The Theme Of Love

'Tis well to wake the theme of Love
When chords of wild ecstatic fire
Fling from the harp, and amply prove
The soul as joyous as the lyre.

Such theme is blissful when the heart
Warms with the precious name we pour;
When our deep pulses glow and start
Before the idol we adore.

Sing ye, whose doting eyes behold –
Whose ears can drink the dear one's tone;
Whose hands may press, whose arms may fold–
The prized, the beautiful, thine own!

But should the ardent hopes of youth
Have cherished dreams that darkly fled;
Should passion, purity, and truth,
Live on, despairing o'er the dead:

Should we have heard some sweet voice hushed,
Breathing our name in latest vow;
Should our fast heavy tears have gushed
Above a cold, yet worshipped brow:

Oh! say, then, can the minstrel choose
The theme that gods and mortals praise?
No, no; the spirit will refuse,
And sadly shun such raptured lays.

For who can bear to touch the string
That yields but anguish in its strain;
Whose lightest notes have power to wring
The keenest pangs from breast and brain?

'Sing ye of Love in words that burn?'
Is what full many a lip will ask;
But love the dead, and ye will learn
Such bidding is no gentle task.

Oh! pause in mercy, ere ye blame
The one who lends not Love his lyre;
That which *ye* deem ethereal flame
May be to *him* a torture pyre.

Eliza Cook

Helas!

To drift with every passion till my soul
Is a stringed lute on which all winds can play,
Is it for this that I have given away
Mine ancient wisdom, and austere control?
Methinks my life is a twice-written scroll
Scrawled over on some boyish holiday
With idle songs for pipe and virelay,
Which do but mar the secret of the whole.
Surely there was a time I might have trod
The sunlit heights, and from life's dissonance
Struck one clear chord to reach the ears of God:
Is that time dead? Lo! with a little rod
I did but touch the honey of romance –
And must I lose a soul's inheritance?

Oscar Wilde

On The Death Of Ianthe

To my ninth decade I have tottered on,
And no soft arm bends now my steps to steady;
She, who once led me where she would, is gone,
So when he calls me, Death shall find me ready.

Walter Savage Landor

St Valentine's Day

To-day, all day, I rode upon the down,
With hounds and horsemen, a brave company.
On this side in its glory lay the sea,
On that the Sussex weald, a sea of brown.

The wind was light, and brightly the sun shone,
And still we galloped on from gorse to gorse:
And once, when checked, a thrush sang, and my horse
Pricked his quick ears as to a sound unknown.
I knew the Spring was come. I knew it even
Better than all by this, that through my chase
In bush and stone and hill and sea and heaven
I seemed to see and follow still your face.
Your face my quarry was. For it I rode,
My horse a thing of wings, myself a god.

Wilfrid Scawen Blunt

The Mermaidens' Vesper-Hymn

Troop home to silent grots and caves!
Troop home! and mimic as you go
The mournful winding of the waves
Which to their dark abysses flow.

At this sweet hour, all things beside
In amorous pairs to covert creep;
The swans that brush the evening tide
Homeward in snowy couples keep.

In his green den the murmuring seal
Close by his sleek companion lies;
While singly we to bedward steal,
And close in fruitless sleep our eyes.

In bowers of love men take their rest,
In loveless bowers we sigh alone,
With bosom friends are others blest, –
But we have none! but we have none!

George Darley

My Wife

Trusty, dusky, vivid, true,
With eyes of gold and bramble-dew,
Steel-true and blade-straight,
The great artificer
Made my mate.

Honour, anger, valour, fire,
A love that life could never tire,
Death quench or evil stir,
The mighty master
Gave to her.

Teacher, tender, comrade, wife,
A fellow-farer true through life,
Heart-whole and soul-free,
The august father
Gave to me.

Robert Louis Stevenson

Did Not

'Twas a new feeling – something more
Than we had dared to own before,
Which then we hid not:
We saw it in each other's eye;
And wished, in every half-breathed sigh,
To speak, but did not.

She felt my lips impassioned touch –
'Twas the first time I dared so much,
And yet she chid not;
But whispered o'er my burning brow,
'Oh, do you doubt I love you now?'
Sweet soul! I did not.

Warmly I felt her bosom thrill,
I pressed it closer, closer still,
Though gently bid not;
Till – oh! the world hath seldom heard
Of lovers, who so nearly erred,
And yet, who did not.

Thomas Moore

The Spousal Time Of May

'Twas when the spousal time of May
Hangs all the hedge with bridal wreaths,
And air's so sweet the bosom gay
Gives thanks for every breath it breathes;
When like to like is gladly moved,
And each thing joins in Spring's refrain,
'Let those love now who never loved;
'Let those who have loved love again;'
That I, in whom the sweet time wrought,
Lay stretched within a lonely glade,
Abandoned to delicious thought,
Beneath the softly twinkling shade.
The leaves, all stirring, mimicked well
A neighbouring rush of rivers cold,
And, as the sun or shadow fell,
So these were green and those were gold;
In dim recesses hyacinths drooped,
And breadths of primrose lit the air,
Which, wandering through the woodland, stooped
And gathered perfumes here and there;
Upon the spray the squirrel swung,
And careless songsters, six or seven,
Sang lofty songs the leaves among,
Fit for their only listener, Heaven.

Coventry Patmore

Lucy's Flittin'

'Twas when the wan leaf frae the birk tree was fa'in,
And Martinmas d'owie had wound up the year,
That Lucy rowed up her wee kist wi' her a' in't,
And left her auld maister and neebours sae dear;
For Lucy had served in the glen a' the simmer;
She cam' there afore the flower bloomed on the pea;
An orphan was she, and they had been kind till her,
Sure that was the thing brocht the tear to her e'e.

She gaed by the stable where Jamie was stannin';
Richt sair was his kind heart, the flittin' to see;
'Fare ye weel, Lucy!' quo' Jamie, and ran in;
The gatherin' tears trickled fast frae his e'e.
As down the burn-side she gaed slow wi' the flittin',
'Fare ye weel, Lucy!' was ilka bird's sang;
She heard the craw sayin't, high on the tree sittin',
And robin was chirpin't the brown leaves amang.

Oh, what is't that pits my puir heart in a flutter?
And what gars the tears come sae fast to my e'e?
If I wasna ettled to be ony better,
Then what gars me wish ony better to be?
I'm just like a lammie that loses its mither;
Nae mither or friend the puir lammie can see;
I fear I ha'e tint my puir heart a' thegither,
Nae wonder the tears fa' sae fast frae my e'e.

Wi' the rest o' my claes I ha'e rowed up the ribbon,
The bonnie blue ribbon that Jamie ga'e me;
Yestreen, when he ga'e me't, and saw I was sabbin',
I'll never forget the wae blink o' his e'e.
Though now he said naething but 'Fare ye weel, Lucy!'
It made me I could neither speak, hear, nor see;
He could nae say mair but just, 'Fare ye weel, Lucy!'
Yet that I will mind till the day that I dee.

William Laidlaw

Reason

Unloved I love, unwept I weep,
Grief I restrain, hope I repress;
Vain is this anguish, fixed and deep,
Vainer desires or means of bliss.

My life is cold, love's fire being dead;
That fire self-kindled, self-consumed;
What living warmth erewhile it shed,
Now to how drear extinction doomed!

Devoid of charm how could I dream
My unasked love would e'er return?
What fate, what influence lit the flame
I still feel inly, deeply burn?

Alas! there are those who should not love;
I to this dreary band belong;
This knowing let me henceforth prove
Too wise to list delusion's song.

No, Syren! Beauty is not mine;
Affection's joy I ne'er shall know;
Lonely will be my life's decline,
Even as my youth is lonely now.

Come Reason – Science – Learning – Thought –
To you my heart I dedicate;
I have a faithful subject brought:
Faithful because most desolate.

Fear not a wandering, feeble mind:
Stern Sovereign, it is all your own
To crush, to cheer, to loose, to bind;
Unclaimed, unshared, it seeks your throne.

Soft may the breeze of summer blow,
Sweetly its sun in valleys shine;
All earth around with love may glow, –
No warmth shall reach this heart of mine.

Vain boast and false! Even now the fire
Though smothered, slacked, repelled, is burning
At my life's source; and stronger, higher,
Waxes the spirit's trampled yearning.

It wakes but to be crushed again:
Faint I will not nor yield to sorrow;
Conflict and force will quell the brain;
Doubt not I shall be strong to-morrow.

Have I not fled that I may conquer?
Crost the dark sea in firmest faith
That I at last might plant my anchor
Where love cannot prevail to death?

Charlotte Brontë

Waking

Waking is wonder; summer airs
Ripple the wheat-field, where a crew
Of winged sweet thieves in flights, in pairs,
Their knavish craft pursue.

They dip, lurk, eddy, swing and sway
Upon the stalk – glad, wrangling throats;
While silent to the wind-flecked bay
Glide home the pilchard-boats.

Waking is infant joy new born;
And how should wonder e'er be dead
For me, who lean toward the morn
Across so dear a head?

Edward Dowden

A Dream

Was it a dream? We sailed, I thought we sailed,
Martin and I, down a green Alpine stream,
Bordered, each bank, with pines; the morning sun,
On the wet umbrage of their glossy tops,
On the red pinings of their forest-floor,
Drew a warm scent abroad; behind the pines
The mountain-skirts, with all their sylvan change
Of bright-leafed chestnuts and mossed walnut-trees
And the frail scarlet-berried ash, began.
Swiss chalets glittered on the dewy slopes,
And from some swarded shelf, high up, there came
Notes of wild pastoral music – over all
Ranged, diamond-bright, the eternal wall of snow.
Upon the mossy rocks at the stream's edge,
Backed by the pines, a plank-built cottage stood,
Bright in the sun; the climbing gourd-plant's leaves
Muffled its walls, and on the stone-strewn roof
Lay the warm golden gourds; golden, within,
Under the eaves, peered rows of Indian corn.
We shot beneath the cottage with the stream.
On the brown, rude-carved balcony, two forms
Came forth – Olivia's, Marguerite! and thine.
Clad were they both in white, flowers in their breast;
Straw hats bedecked their heads, with ribbons blue,
Which danced, and on their shoulders, fluttering,
    played.
They saw us, they conferred; their bosoms heaved,

And more than mortal impulse filled their eyes.
Their lips moved; their white arms, waved eagerly,
Flashed once, like falling streams; we rose, we gazed.
One moment, on the rapid's top, our boat
Hung poised – and then the darting river of Life
(Such now, methought, it was), the river of Life,
Loud thundering, bore us by; swift, swift it foamed,
Black under cliffs it raced, round headlands shone.
Soon the planked cottage by the sun-warmed pines
Faded – the moss – the rocks; us burning plains,
Bristled with cities, us the sea received.

Matthew Arnold

The Harlot's House

We caught the tread of dancing feet,
We loitered down the moonlit street,
And stopped beneath the harlot's house.

Inside, above the din and fray,
We heard the loud musicians play
The 'Treues Liebes Herz' of Strauss.

Like strange mechanical grotesques,
Making fantastic arabesques,
The shadows raced across the blind.

We watched the ghostly dancers spin
To sound of horn and violin,
Like black leaves wheeling in the wind.

Like wire-pulled automatons,
Slim silhouetted skeletons
Went sidling through the slow quadrille.

They took each other by the hand,
And danced a stately saraband;
Their laughter echoed thin and shrill.

Sometimes a clockwork puppet pressed
A phantom lover to her breast,
Sometimes they seemed to try to sing.

Sometimes a horrible marionette
Came out, and smoked its cigarette
Upon the steps like a live thing.

Then, turning to my love, I said,
'The dead are dancing with the dead,
The dust is whirling with the dust.'

But she – she heard the violin,
And left my side, and entered in:
Love passed into the house of lust.

Then suddenly the tune went false,
The dancers wearied of the waltz,
The shadows ceased to wheel and whirl.

And down the long and silent street,
The dawn, with silver-sandaled feet,
Crept like a frightened girl.

Oscar Wilde

Bridal Song

By female voices
We have bathed, where none have seen us,
In the lake and in the fountain,
Underneath the charmed statue
Of the timid, bending Venus,
When the water-nymphs were counting
In the waves the stars of night,
And whose maidens started at you,
Your limbs shone through so soft and bright.
But no secrets dare we tell,
For thy slaves unlace thee,
And he who shall embrace thee,
Waits to try thy beauty's spell.

By male voices
We have crowned thee queen of women,
Since love's love, the rose, hath kept her
Court within thy lips and blushes,
And thine eye, in beauty swimming,
Kissing, rendered up the sceptre,
At whose touch the startled soul
Like an ocean bounds and gushes,
And spirits bend at thy control.
But no secrets dare we tell,
For thy slaves unlace thee,
And he, who shall embrace thee,
Is at hand, and so farewell.

Thomas Lovell Beddoes

A Denial

We have met late – it is too late to meet,
O friend, not more than friend!
Death's forecome shroud is tangled round my feet,
And if I step or stir, I touch the end.
In this last jeopardy
Can I approach thee, I, who cannot move?
How shall I answer thy request for love?
Look in my face and see.

I love thee not, I dare not love thee! go
In silence; drop my hand.
If thou seek roses, seek them where they blow
In garden-alleys, not in desert-sand.
Can life and death agree,
That thou shouldst stoop thy song to my complaint?
I cannot love thee. If the word is faint,
Look in my face and see.

I might have loved thee in some former days,
Oh, then, my spirits had leapt
As now they sink, at hearing thy love-praise.
Before these faded cheeks were overwept,
Had this been asked of me,
To love thee with my whole strong heart and head, –
I should have said still . . . yes, but *smiled* and said,
'Look in my face and see!'

But now . . . God sees me, God, who took my heart
And drowned it in life's surge.
In all your wide warm earth I have no part –
A light song overcomes me like a dirge.
Could Love's great harmony
The saints keep step to when their bonds are loose,
Not weigh me down? am *I* a wife to choose?
Look in my face and see.

While I behold, as plain as one who dreams,
Some woman of full worth,
Whose voice, as cadenced as a silver stream's,
Shall prove the fountain-soul which sends it forth;
One younger, more thought-free
And fair and gay, than I, thou must forget,
With brighter eyes than these . . . which are not wet . . .
Look in my face and see!

So farewell thou, whom I have known too late
To let thee come so near.
Be counted happy while men call thee great,
And one belovèd woman feels thee dear! –
Not I! – that cannot be.
I am lost, I am changed, – I must go farther, where
The change shall take me worse, and no one dare
Look in my face to see.

Meantime I bless thee. By these thoughts of mine
I bless thee from all such!
I bless thy lamp to oil, thy cup to wine,
Thy hearth to joy, thy hand to an equal touch
Of loyal troth. For me,
I love thee not, I love thee not! – away!
Here's no more courage in my soul to say
'Look in my face and see.'

Elizabeth Barrett Browning

In Kerry

We heard the thrushes by the shore and sea,
And saw the golden stars' nativity,
Then round we went the lane by Thomas Flynn,
Across the church where bones lie out and in;
And there I asked beneath a lonely cloud
Of strange delight, with one bird singing loud,
What change you'd wrought in graveyard, rock and sea,
This new wild paradise to wake for me. . .
Yet knew no more than knew these merry sins
Had built this stack of thigh-bones, jaws and shins.

J. M. Synge

On The Departure Platform

We kissed at the barrier; and passing through
She left me, and moment by moment got
Smaller and smaller, until to my view
She was but a spot;

A wee white spot of muslin fluff
That down the diminishing platform bore
Through hustling crowds of gentle and rough
To the carriage door.

Under the lamplight's fitful glowers,
Behind dark groups from far and near,
Whose interests were apart from ours,
She would disappear,

Then show again, till I ceased to see
That flexible form, that nebulous white;
And she who was more than my life to me
Had vanished quite. . . .

We have penned new plans since that fair fond day,
And in season she will appear again –
Perhaps in the same soft white array –
But never as then!

– 'And why, young man, must eternally fly
A joy you'll repeat, if you love her well?'
– O friend, nought happens twice thus; why,
I cannot tell!

Thomas Hardy

Adam's Curse

We sat together at one summer's end,
That beautiful mild woman, your close friend,
And you and I, and talked of poetry.
I said: 'A line will take us hours maybe;
Yet if it does not seem a moment's thought,
Our stitching and unstitching has been naught.
Better go down upon your marrow-bones
And scrub a kitchen pavement, or break stones
Like an old pauper, in all kinds of weather;
For to articulate sweet sounds together
Is to work harder than all these, and yet
Be thought an idler by the noisy set
Of bankers, schoolmasters, and clergymen
The martyrs call the world.'

        And thereupon
That beautiful mild woman for whose sake
There's many a one shall find out all heartache
On finding that her voice is sweet and low
Replied: 'To be born woman is to know –
Although they do not talk of it at school –
That we must labour to be beautiful.'

I said: 'It's certain there is no fine thing
Since Adam's fall but needs much labouring.
There have been lovers who thought love should be
So much compounded of high courtesy
That they would sigh and quote with learned looks
Precedents out of beautiful old books;
Yet now it seems an idle trade enough.'

We sat grown quiet at the name of love;
We saw the last embers of daylight die,
And in the trembling blue-green of the sky
A moon, worn as if it had been a shell
Washed by time's waters as they rose and fell
About the stars and broke in days and years.

I had a thought for no one's but your ears:
That you were beautiful, and that I strove
To love you in the old high way of love;
That it had all seemed happy, and yet we'd grown
As weary-hearted as that hollow moon.

W. B. Yeats

Isolation. To Marguerite

We were apart; yet, day by day
I bade my heart more constant be.
I bade it keep the world away,
And grow a home for only thee;
Nor feared but thy love likewise grew,
Like mine, each day, more tried, more true.

The fault was grave! I might have known,
What far too soon, alas! I learned –
The heart can bind itself alone,
And faith may oft be unreturned.
Self-swayed our feelings ebb and swell –
Thou lovest no more; – Farewell! Farewell!

Farewell! – and thou, thou lonely heart,
Which never yet without remorse
Even for a moment didst depart
From thy remote and spheréd course
To haunt the place where passions reign –
Back to thy solitude again!

Back! with the conscious thrill of shame
Which Luna felt, that summer-night,
Flash through her pure immortal frame,
When she forsook the starry height
To hang over Endymion's sleep
Upon the pine-grown Latmian steep.

Yet she, chaste queen, had never proved
How vain a thing is mortal love,
Wandering in Heaven, far removed.
But thou hast long had place to prove
This truth – to prove, and make thine own:
'Thou hast been, shalt be, art, alone.'

Or, if not quite alone, yet they
Which touch thee are unmating things –
Ocean and clouds and night and day;
Lorn autumns and triumphant springs;
And life, and others' joy and pain,
And love, if love, of happier men.

Of happier men – for they, at least,
Have *dreamed* two human hearts might blend
In one, and were through faith released
From isolation without end
Prolonged; nor knew, although not less
Alone than thou, their loneliness.

Matthew Arnold

A Woman's Last Word

Well – the links are broken,
All is past;
This farewell, when spoken,
Is the last.
I have tried and striven
All in vain;
Such bonds must be riven,
Spite of pain,
And never, never, never
Knit again.

So I tell you plainly,
It must be:
I shall try, not vainly,
To be free;
Truer, happier chances
Wait me yet,
While you, through fresh fancies,
Can forget; –
And life has nobler uses
Than Regret.

All past words retracing,
One by one,
Does not help effacing
What is done.
Let it be. Oh, stronger
Links can break!
Had we dreamed still longer
We could wake, –
Yet let us part in kindness
For Love's sake.

Bitterness and sorrow
Will at last,
In some bright to-morrow,

Heal their past;
But future hearts will never
Be as true
As mine was – is ever,
Dear, for you . . .
Then must we part, when loving
As we do?

Adelaide Anne Procter

Durisdeer

We'll meet nae mair at sunset, when the weary day is
    dune,
Nor wander hame thegither, by the lee licht o' the
    mune!
I'll hear your step nae langer amang the dewy corn,
For we'll meet nae mair, my bonniest, either at eve or
    morn.

The yellow broom is waving, abune the sunny brae,
And the rowan berries dancing, where the sparkling
    waters play,
Tho' a' is bright and bonnie, it's an eerie place to me,
For we'll meet nae mair, my dearest, either by burn or
    tree.

Far up into the wild hills, there's a kirkyard auld and
    still,
Where the frosts lie ilka morning, and the mists hang
    low and chill,
And there ye sleep in silence, while I wander here my
    lane,
Till we meet ance mair in Heaven, never to part again!

Lady John Scott

Were You With Me

Were you with me, or I with you,
There's nought, methinks, I might not do;
Could venture here, and venture there,
And never fear, nor ever care.

To things before, and things behind,
Could turn my thoughts, and turn my mind,
On this and that, day after day,
Could care to throw myself away.

Secure, when all was o'er, to find
My proper thought, my perfect mind,
And unimpaired receive anew
My own and better self in you.

Arthur Hugh Clough

Modern Love XXX

What are we first? First, animals; and next
Intelligences at a leap; on whom
Pale lies the distant shadow of the tomb,
And all that draweth on the tomb for text.
Into which state comes Love, the crowning sun:
Beneath whose light the shadow loses form.
We are the lords of life, and life is warm.
Intelligence and instinct now are one.
But nature says: 'My children most they seem
When they least know me: therefore I decree
That they shall suffer.' Swift doth young Love flee,
And we stand wakened, shivering from our dream.
Then if we study Nature we are wise.
Thus do the few who live but with the day:
The scientific animals are they. –
Lady, this is my sonnet to your eyes.

George Meredith

The Gift

What can I give you, my lord, my lover,
You who have given the world to me,
Showed me the light and the joy that cover
The wild sweet earth and the restless sea?

All that I have are gifts of your giving –
If I give them again, you would find them old,
And your soul would weary of always living
Before the mirror my life would hold.

What shall I give you, my lord, my lover?
The gift that breaks the heart in me:
I bid you awake at dawn and discover
I have gone my way and left you free.

Sara Teesdale

What Have I Lost?

(From A Woman's Sonnets VI)

What have I lost? The faith I had that right
Must surely prove itself than ill more strong.
For all my prayers and efforts had no might
To save me, when the trial came, from wrong.
And lost the days when with untroubled eyes
Scorning deceit, I could hold up my head.
I lead a double life – myself despise
And fear each day to have my secret read.
No longer will the loved and lost I mourn
Come in my sleep to breathe a blessed word.
Tossing I lie, and restless and forlorn,
And their dear memory pierces like a sword.
In thy dear presence only have I rest.
To thee alone naught needs to be confessed.

Augusta, Lady Gregory

Confessions

'What is he buzzing in my ears?
'Now that I come to die,
'Do I view the world as a vale of tears?'
Ah, reverend sir, not I!

What I viewed there once, what I view again
Where the physic bottles stand
On the table's edge, – is a suburb lane,
With a wall, to my bedside hand.

That lane sloped, much as the bottles do,
From a house you could descry
O'er the garden wall: is the curtain blue
Or green to a healthy eye?

To mine, it serves for the old June weather
Blue above land and wall;
And that farthest bottle labelled 'Ether'
Is the house o'ertopping all.

At a terrace, somewhere near the stopper,
There watched for me, one June,
A girl: I know, sir, it's improper,
My poor mind's out of tune.

Only, there was a way . . . you crept
Close by the side, to dodge
Eyes in the house, two eyes except:
They styled their house 'The Lodge.'

What right had a lounger up their lane?
But, by creeping very close,
With the good wall's help, – their eyes might strain
And stretch themselves to Oes,

Yet never catch her and me together,
As she left the attic, there,
By the rim of the bottle labelled 'Ether',
And stole from stair to stair,

And stood by the rose-wreathed gate
Alas,
We loved, sir – used to meet:
How sad and bad and mad it was –
But then, how it was sweet!

Robert Browning

From Love In The Valley

When at dawn she sighs, and like an infant to the
    window
Turns grave eyes craving light, released from dreams,
Beautiful she looks, like a white water-lily
Bursting out of bud in havens of the streams.
When from bed she rises clothed from neck to ankle
In her long nightgown sweet as boughs of May,
Beautiful she looks, like a tall garden-lily
Pure from the night, and splendid for the day.

Mother of the dews, dark eye-lashed twilight,
Low-lidded twilight, o'er the valley's brim,
Rounding on thy breast sings the dew-delighted
    skylark,
Clear as though the dewdrops had their voice in him,
Hidden where the rose-flush drinks the rayless planet,
Fountain-full he pours the spraying fountain showers.
Let me hear her laughter, I would have her ever
Cool as dew in twilight, the lark above the flowers.

George Meredith

Song

When I am dead, my dearest,
Sing no sad songs for me;
Plant thou no roses at my head,
Nor shady cypress tree:
Be the green grass above me
With showers and dewdrops wet:
And if thou wilt, remember,
And if thou wilt, forget.

I shall not see the shadows,
I shall not feel the rain:
I shall not hear the nightingale
Sing on as if in pain:
And dreaming through the twilight
That doth not rise nor set,
Haply I may remember,
And haply may forget.

Christina Rossetti

When I Set Out For Lyonnesse

When I set out for Lyonnesse,
A hundred miles away,
The rime was on the spray,
And starlight lit my lonesomeness
When I set out for Lyonnesse
A hundred miles away.

What would bechance at Lyonnesse
While I should sojourn there
No prophet durst declare,
Nor did the wisest wizard guess
What would bechance at Lyonnesse
While I should sojourn there.

When I came back from Lyonnesse
With magic in my eyes,
All marked with mute surmise
My radiance rare and fathomless,
When I came back from Lyonnesse
With magic in my eyes!

Thomas Hardy

He Remembers Forgotten Beauty

When my arms wrap you round I press
My heart upon the loveliness
That has long faded from the world;
The jewelled crowns that kings have hurled
In shadowy pools, when armies fled;
The love-tales wrought with silken thread
By dreaming ladies upon cloth
That has made fat the murderous moth;
The roses that of old times were
Woven by ladies in their hair,
The dew-cold lilies ladies bore
Through many a sacred corridor
Where such grey clouds of incense rose
That only God's eyes did not close:
For that pale breast and lingering hand
Came from a more dream-heavy land,
A more dream-heavy hour than this;
And when you sigh from kiss to kiss
I hear white Beauty sighing, too,
For hours when all must fade like dew,
But flame on flame, and deep on deep,
Throne over throne where in half sleep,
Their swords upon their iron knees,
Brood her high lonely mysteries.

W. B. Yeats

Absence

When my love was away,
Full three days were not sped,
I caught my fancy astray
Thinking if she were dead,

And I alone, alone:
It seemed in my misery
In all the world was none
Ever so lone as I.

I wept; but it did not shame
Nor comfort my heart: away
I rode as I might, and came
To my love at close of day.

The sight of her stilled my fears,
My fairest-hearted love:
And yet in her eyes were tears:
Which when I questioned of,

'O now thou art come,' she cried,
''Tis fled: but I thought to-day
I never could here abide,
If thou wert longer away.'

Robert Bridges

Lines

*On Reading with Difficulty Some of Schiller's Early Love
Poems*

When of thy loves, and happy heavenly dreams
Of early life, O Bard! I strive to read,
Thy foreign utterance a riddle seems,
And hardly can I hold thy thought's bright thread.
When of the maiden's guilt, the mother's woe,
And the dark mystery of death and shame,
Thou speakest – then thy terrible numbers flow
As if the tongue we think in were the same.
Ah wherefore! but because all joy and love
Speak unfamiliar, unknown words to me,
A spirit of wishful wonder they may move,
Dreams of what might – but yet shall never be.
But the sharp cry of pain – the bitter moan
Of trust deceived – the horrible despair
Of hope and love for ever overthrown –
These strains of thine need no interpreter.
Ah! 'tis my native tongue! and howsoe'er
In foreign accents writ, that I did ne'er
Or speak, or hear, a woman's agony
Still utters a familiar voice to me.

Fanny Kemble

When Our Two Souls Stand Up

(Sonnets from The Portuguese XXII)

When our two souls stand up erect and strong,
Face to face, silent, drawing nigh and nigher,
Until the lengthening wings break into fire
At either curvèd point, – what bitter wrong
Can the earth do to us, that we should not long
Be here contented! Think. In mounting higher,

The angels would press on us, and aspire
To drop some golden orb of perfect song
Into our deep, dear silence. Let us stay
Rather on earth, Belovèd, – where the unfit
Contrarious moods of men recoil away
And isolate pure spirits, and permit
A place to stand and love in for a day,
With darkness and the death-hour rounding it.

Elizabeth Barrett Browning

Hereafter

When you and I have played the little hour,
Have seen the tall subaltern Life to Death
Yield up his sword; and, smiling, draw the breath,
The first long breath of freedom; when the flower
Of Recompense hath fluttered to our feet,
As to an actor's; and, the curtain down,
We turn to face each other all alone –
Alone, we two, who never yet did meet,
Alone, and absolute, and free: O then,
O then, most dear, how shall be told the tale?
Clasped hands, pressed lips, and so clasped hands
    again;
No words. But as the proud wind fills the sail,
My love to yours shall reach, then one deep moan
Of joy, and then our infinite Alone.

Sir Gilbert Parker

When You Are Old

When you are old and grey and full of sleep
And nodding by the fire, take down this book,
And slowly read, and dream of the soft look
Your eyes had once, and of their shadows deep;

How many loved your moments of glad grace,
And loved your beauty with love false or true;
But one man loved the pilgrim soul in you,
And loved the sorrows of your changing face.

And bending down beside the glowing bars,
Murmur, a little sadly, how love fled
And paced upon the mountains overhead,
And hid his face amid a crowd of stars.

W. B. Yeats

The Lapful Of Nuts
(A Translation from The Irish)

When'er I see soft hazel eyes
And nut-brown curls,
I think of those bright days I spent
Among the Limerick girls;
When up through Cratla woods I went,
Nutting with thee;
And we plucked the glossy clustering fruit
From many a bending tree.

Beneath the hazel boughs we sat,
Thou, love, and I,
And the gathered nuts lay in thy lap,
Beneath thy downcast eye:
But little we thought of the store we'd won,

I, love, or thou;
For our hearts were full, and we dare not own
The love that's spoken now.

Oh, there's wars for willing hearts in Spain,
And high Germanie!
And I'll come back, ere long, again,
With knightly fame and fee:
And I'll come back, if I ever come back,
Faithful to thee,
That sat with thy white lap full of nuts
Beneath the hazel tree.

Sir Samuel Ferguson

A Separation Deed

Whereas we twain, who still are bound for life,
Who took each other for better and for worse,
And now plunged deep in hate and bitter strife,
And all our former love is grown a curse;
So that 'twere better, doubtless, we should be
In loneliness, so that we were apart,
Nor in each other's changed eyes looking, see
The cold reflection of an alien heart;
To this insensate parchment we reveal
Our joint despair, and seal it with our seal.

Forgetting the dear days not long ago,
When we walked slow by starlight through the corn:
Forgetting, since our hard fate wills it so,
All but our parted lives and souls forlorn;
Forgetting the sweet fetters strong to bind
Which childish fingers forge, and baby smiles,
Our common pride to watch the growing mind,
Our common joy in childhood's simple wiles,
The common tears we shed, the kiss we gave,
Standing beside the open little grave.

Forgetting these and more, if to forget
Be possible, as we would fain indeed.
And if the past be not too deeply set
In our two hearts, with roots that, touched, will bleed
Yet, could we cheat by any pretext fair
The world, if not ourselves – 'twere so far well –
We would not put our bonds from us, and bare
To careless eyes the secrets of our hell;
So this indenture witnesseth that we,
As follows here, do solemnly agree.

We will take each our own, and will abide
Separate from bed and board for all our life;
Whatever chance of weal or woe betide,
Naught shall re-knit the husband and the wife.
Though one grow gradually poor and weak,
The other, lapt in luxury, will not heed;
Though one, in mortal pain, the other seek,
The other may not answer to the need;
We, who through long years did together rest
In wedlock, heart to heart, and breast to breast.

One shall the daughter take, and one the boy, –
Poor boy, who shall not hear his mother's name,
Nor feel her kiss; poor girl, for whom the joy
Of her sire's smile is changed for sullen shame:
Brother and sister, who, if they should meet,
With faces strange, amid the careless crowd,
Will feel their hearts beat with no quicker beat,
Nor inward voice of kinship calling loud:
Two widowed lives, whose fullness may not come;
Two orphan lives, knowing but half of home.

We have not told the tale, nor will, indeed,
Of dissonance, whether cruel wrong or crime,
Or sum of petty injuries which breed
The hate of hell when multiplied by time,
Dishonour, falsehood, jealous fancies, blcws,
Which in one moment wedded souls can sunder;
But, since our yoke intolerable grows,
Therefore we set out seals and souls as under:
Witness the powers of wrong and hate and death.
And this indenture also witnesseth.

Sir Lewis Morris

Lost Love

Who wins his love shall lose her,
Who loses her shall gain,
For still the spirit woos her,
A soul without a stain;
And memory still pursues her
With longings not in vain!

He loses her who gains her,
Who watches day by day
The dust of time that stains her,
The griefs that leave her gray –
The flesh that yet enchains her
Whose grace hath passed away!

Oh, happier he who gains not
The love some seem to gain:
The joy that custom stains not
Shall still with him remain;
The loveliness that wanes not,
The love, that ne'er can wane.

In dreams she grows not older
The lands of dream among;
Though all the world wax colder,
Though all the songs be sung,
In dreams doth he behold her
Still fair and kind and young.

Andrew Lang

Why?

Why did you come, with your enkindled eyes
And mountain-look, across my lower way.
And take the vague dishonour from my day
By luring me from paltry things, to rise
And stand beside you, waiting wistfully
The looming of a larger destiny?

Why did you with strong fingers fling aside
The gates of possibility, and say
With vital voice the words I dream to-day?
Before, I was not much unsatisfied:
But since a god has touched me and departed,
I run through every temple, broken-hearted.

Mary Webb

The Married Lover

Why, having won her, do I woo?
Because her spirit's vestal grace
Provokes me always to pursue,
But, spirit-like, eludes embrace;
Because her womanhood is such
That, as on court-days subjects kiss
The Queen's hand, yet so near a touch
Affirms no mean familiarness;
Nay, rather marks more fair the height
Which can with safety so neglect
To dread, as lower ladies might,
That grace could meet with disrespect;
Thus she with happy favour feeds
Allegiance from a love so high
That thence no false conceit proceeds
Of difference bridged, or state put by;
Because although in act and word
As lowly as a wife can be,
Her manners, when they call me lord,
Remind me 'tis by courtesy;
Not with her least consent of will,
Which would my proud affection hurt,
But by the noble style that still
Imputes an unattained desert;
Because her gay and lofty brows,
When all is won which hope can ask,
Reflect a light of hopeless snows
That bright in virgin ether bask;
Because, though free of the outer court
I am, this Temple keeps its shrine
Sacred to Heaven; because, in short,
She's not and never can be mine.

Coventry Patmore

No Second Troy

Why should I blame her that she filled my days
With misery, or that she would of late
Have taught to ignorant men most violent ways,
Or hurled the little streets upon the great,
Had they but courage equal to desire?
What could have made her peaceful with a mind
That nobleness made simple as a fire,
With beauty like a tightened bow, a kind
That is not natural in an age like this,
Being high and solitary and most stern?
Why, what could she have done, being what she is?
Was there another Troy for her to burn?

W. B. Yeats

Wild Words I Write
(From A Woman's Sonnets XI)

Wild words I write, wild words of love and pain
To lay within thy hand before we part,
For now that we may never meet again
I would make bare to thee my inmost heart.
For when I speak you answer with a jest
Or laugh and break the sentence with a kiss
And so my love is never half confessed
Nor have I told thee what has been my bliss.
And when the darkness and the clouds prevail
And I begin to know what I have lost
I would not vex thee with so sad a tale
Or tell how all too dear my love has cost.
But now the time has come when I must go
The tumults and the joy I fain would show.

Augusta, Lady Gregory

An Invite to Eternity

Wilt thou go with me sweet maid
Say maiden wilt thou go with me
Through the valley depths of shade
Of night and dark obscurity
Where the path hath lost its way
Where the sun forgets the day
Where there's nor life nor light to see
Sweet maiden wilt thou go with me.

Where stones will turn to flooding streams
Where plains will rise like ocean waves
Where life will fade like visioned dreams
And mountains darken into caves
Say maiden wilt thou go with me
Through this sad non-identity
Where parents live and are forgot
And sisters live and know us not.

Say maiden wilt thou go with me
In this strange death of life to be
To live in death and be the same
Without this life or home or name
At once to be and not to be
That was and is not – yet to see
Things pass like shadows – and the sky
Above, below, around us lie.

The land of shadows wilt thou trace
And look nor know each other's face
The present mixed with reasons gone
And past and present all as one
Say maiden can thy life be led
To join the living with the dead?
Then trace thy footsteps on with me
We're wed to one eternity.

John Clare

Winter Winds Cold And Blea

Winter winds cold and blea
Chilly blows o'er the lea:
Wander not out to me,
Jenny so fair,
Wait in thy cottage free.
I will be there.

Wait in thy cushioned chair
Wi' thy white bosom bare.
Kisses are sweetest there:
Leave it for me.
Free from the chilly air
I will meet thee.

How sweet can courting prove,
How can I kiss my love
Muffled in hat and glove
From the chill air?
Quaking beneath the grove,
What love is there!

Lay by thy woollen vest,
Drape no cloak o'er thy breast,
Where my hand oft hath pressed
Pin nothing there:
Where my head droops to rest,
Leave its bed bare.

John Clare

A Farewell

With all my will, but much against my heart,
We two now part.
My Very Dear,
Our solace is, the sad road lies so clear.
It needs no art,
With faint, averted feet
An many a tear,
In our opposed paths to persevere.
Go thou to East, I West,
We will not say
There's any hope, it is so far away.
But O my Best,
When the one darling of our widowhead,
The nursling Grief,
Is dead,
And no dews blur our eyes
To see the peach-bloom come in evening skies,
Perchance we may,
Where now this night is day,
And even through faith of still averted feet,
Making full circle of our banishment,
Amazed meet;
The bitter journey to the bourne so sweet
Seasoning the termless feast of our content
With tears of recognition never dry.

Coventry Patmore

Mariana

'Mariana in the moated grange.'
Measure for Measure

With blackest moss the flower-plots
Were thickly crusted, one and all;
The rusted nails fell from the knots
That held the pear to the gable wall.
The broken sheds looked sad and strange:
Unlifted was the clinking latch;
Weeded and worn the ancient thatch
Upon the lonely moated grange.
She only said, 'My life is dreary,
He cometh not,' she said;
She said, 'I am aweary, aweary,
I would that I were dead!'

Her tears fell with the dews at even;
Her tears fell ere the dews were dried;
She could not look on the sweet heaven,
Either at morn or eventide.
After the flitting of the bats,
When thickest dark did trance the sky,
She drew her casement curtain by,
And glanced athwart the glooming flats.
She only said, 'The night is dreary;
He cometh not,' she said;
She said, 'I am aweary, aweary,
I would that I were dead!'

Upon the middle of the night,
Waking she heard the nightfowl crow:
The cock sung out an hour ere light:
From the dark fen the oxen's low
Came to her; without hope of change,
In sleep she seemed to walk forlorn,
Till cold winds woke the gray-eyed morn

About the lonely moated grange.
She only said, 'The day is dreary,
He cometh not,' she said;
She said, 'I am aweary, aweary,
I would that I were dead!'

About a stonecast from the wall
A sluice with blackened waters slept,
And o'er it many, round and small,
The clustered marish-mosses crept.
Hard by a poplar shook alway,
All silver-green with gnarléd bark:
For leagues no other tree did mark
The level waste, the rounding gray.
She only said, 'My life is dreary,
He cometh not,' she said;
She said, 'I am aweary, aweary,
I would that I were dead!'

And ever when the moon was low,
And the shrill winds were up and away,
In the white curtain, to and fro,
She saw the gusty shadow sway.
But when the moon was very low,
And wild winds bound within their cell,
The shadow of the poplar fell
Upon her bed, across her brow.
She only said, 'The night is dreary,
He cometh not,' she said;
She said, 'I am aweary, aweary,
I would that I were dead!'

All day within the dreamy house,
The doors upon their hinges creaked;
The blue fly sung in the pane; the mouse
Behind the mouldering wainscot shrieked,
Or from the crevice peered about.
Old faces glimmered through the doors,

Old footsteps trod the upper floors,
Old voices called her from without.
She only said 'My life is dreary,
He cometh not,' she said;
She said, 'I am aweary, aweary,
I would that I were dead!'

The sparrow's chirrup on the roof,
The slow clock ticking, and the sound
Which to the wooing wind aloof
The poplar made, did all confound
Her sense; but most she loathed the hour
When the thick-moted sunbeam lay
Athwart the chambers, and the day
Was sloping toward his western bower.
Then, said she, 'I am very dreary,
He will not come,' she said;
She wept, 'I am aweary, aweary,
Oh God, that I were dead!'

Alfred, Lord Tennyson

The Girl's Lamentation

With grief and mourning I sit to spin;
My Love passed by, and he didn't come in;
He passes by me, both day and night,
And carries off my poor heart's delight.

There is a tavern in yonder town,
My Love goes there and he spends a crown;
He takes a strange girl upon his knee,
And never more gives a thought to me.

Says he, 'We'll wed without loss of time,
And sure our love's but a little crime'; –
My apron-string now it's wearing short,
And my Love he seeks other girls to court.

O with him I'd go if I had my will,
I'd follow him barefoot o'er rock and hill;
I'd never once speak of all my grief
If he'd give me a smile for my heart's relief.

In our wee garden the rose unfolds,
With bachelor's-buttons and marigolds;
I'll tie no posies for dance or fair,
A willow-twig is for me to wear.

For a maid again I can never be,
Till the red rose blooms on the willow tree.
Of such a trouble I've heard them tell,
And now I know what it means full well.

As through the long lonesome night I lie,
I'd give the world if I might but cry;
But I musn't moan there or raise my voice,
And the tears run down without any noise.

And what, O what will my mother say?
She'll wish her daughter was in the clay.
My father will curse me to my face;
The neighbours will know of my black disgrace.

My sister's buried three years, come Lent;
But sure we made far too much lament.
Beside her grave they still say a prayer –
I wish to God 'twas myself was there!

The Candlemas crosses hang near my bed;
To look at them puts me much in dread,
They mark the good time that's gone and past:
It's like this year's one will prove the last.

The oldest cross it's a dusty brown,
But the winter winds didn't shake it down;
The newest cross keeps the colour bright;
When the straw was reaping my heart was light.

The reapers rose with the blink of morn,
And gaily stooked up the yellow corn;
To call them home to the field I'd run,
Through the blowing breeze and the summer sun.

When the straw was weaving my heart was glad,
For neither sin nor shame I had,
In the barn where oat-chaff was flying round,
And the thumping flails made a pleasant sound.

Now summer or winter to me it's one;
But oh! for a day like the time that's gone.
I'd little care was it storm or shrine,
If I had but peace in this heart of mine.

Oh! light and false is a young man's kiss,
And a foolish girl gives her soul for this.
Oh! light and short is the young man's blame,
And a helpless girl has the grief and shame.

To the river-bank once I thought to go,
And cast myself in the stream below;
I thought 'twould carry us far our to sea,
Where they'd never find my poor babe and me.

Sweet Lord, forgive me that wicked mind!
You know I used to be well-inclined.
Oh, take compassion upon my state,
Because my trouble is so very great.

My head turns round with the spinning wheel,
And a heavy cloud on my eyes I feel,
But the worst of all is at my heart's core;
For my innocent days will come back no more.

William Allingham

Without And Within
(Written To Wilfred Blunt In Prison, 1898)

Without the gate, without the gate
The patient fishers antedate
The dawn and watch with eager eyes
The flashing sudden salmon rise
Without the gate, without the gate.

Within the gate, within the gate
A prisoner wakes to poor estate
The barren light of morning falls
Upon the narrow whitened walls
Within the gate, within the gate.

Without the gate, without the gate
Red skirted women rail and rate
Nor Gaelic jests or curses fail
E'en in the shadow of the gaol
Without the gate, without the gate.

Within the gate, within the gate
He sits and ravels out his fate
With patient unaccustomed hands
Touches the malted oakum strands
Within the gate, within the gate.

Without the gate, without the gate
The swallow nestles to his mate
Home hastening nuns the vespers greet
The idler leaves the darkening street
Without the gate, without the gate.

Within the gate, within the gate
What dreams the captive's sleep await!
A couch of honour is his bed
A glory rests about his head
Within the gate, within the gate

Without the gate, without the gate
I early come, I linger late
I wait the blessed hour when he
Shall come and cross the bridge with me
Without the gate, without the gate.

Augusta, Lady Gregory

The Voice

Woman much missed, how you call to me, call to me,
Saying that now you are not as you were
When you had changed from the one who was all to
    me,
But as at first, when our day was fair.

Can it be you that I hear? Let me view you, then,
Standing as when I draw near to the town
Where you would wait for me: yes, as I knew you then,
Even to the original air-blue gown!

Or is it only the breeze, in its listlessness
Travelling across the wet mead to me here,
You being ever consigned to existlessness,
Heard no more again far or near?

Thus I; faltering forward,
Leaves around me falling,
Wind oozing thin through the thorn from norward,
And the woman calling.

Thomas Hardy

To Marguerite – Continued

Yes! in the sea of life enisled,
With echoing straits between us thrown,
Dotting the shoreless watery wild,
We mortal millions live *alone*.
The islands feel the enclasping flow,
And then their endless bounds they know.

But when the moon their hollows lights,
And they are swept by balms of spring,
And in the glens, on starry nights,
The nightingales divinely sing;
And lovely notes, from shore to shore,
Across the sounds and channels pour –

Oh! then a longing like despair
Is to their farthest caverns sent:
For surely once, they feel, we were
Parts of a single continent!
Now round us spreads the watery plain –
Oh might our marges meet again!

Who ordered, that their longing's fire
Should be, as soon as kindled, cooled?
Who renders vain their deep desire? –
A God, a God their severance ruled!
And bade betwixt their shores to be
The unplumbed, salt, estranging sea.

Matthew Arnold

Consolation
(From Fand)

Yes, let us speak, with lips confirming
The inner pledge that eyes reveal –
Bright eyes that death shall dim for ever,
And lips that silence soon shall seal.

Yes, let us make our claim recorded
Against the powers of earth and sky,
And that cold boon their laws award us –
Just once to live and once to die.

Thou sayest that fate is frosty nothing,
But love the flame of souls that are:
'Two spirits approach, and at their touching,
Behold! an everlasting star.'

High thoughts, O love: well, let us speak them!
Yet bravely face at least this fate:
To know the dreams of us that dream them
On blind, unknowing things await.

If years from winter's chill recover,
If fields are green and rivers run,
If thou and I behold each other,
Hangs it not all on yonder sun?

So while that mighty lord is gracious
With prodigal beams to flood the skies,
Let us be glad that he can spare us
The light to kindle lovers' eyes.

And die assured, should life's new wonder
In any world our slumbers break,
These the first words that each will utter:
'Beloved, art thou too awake?'

William Larminie

Yestreen I Roamed By Jedwater

Yestreen I roamed by Jedwater,
When the sun was set and the dew was doun,
An' there was a sang in Jedwater,
An' my Ailie's name was its tune.
It sang o' her een, it sang o' her hair,
An' it sang o' her neck o' the lily fine;
But aye the sweetest it sang o' her heart,
My Ailie's heart that is mine!

It's up an' doun by Jedwater
I gaed and listened that ae sweet tune,
O it's up and doun by Jedwater,
Till it glentit under the mune.
O her deep, deep een! O her dark, dark hair!
And her lip that is red as the bluid-red wine!
But sing, sweet River, sing aye o' her heart –
My Ailie's heart that is mine!

Thomas Davidson

Affinity

You and I have found the secret way,
None can bar our love or say us nay:
All the world may stare and never know
You and I are twined together so.

You and I for all his vaunted width
Know the Giant Space is but a myth;
Over miles and miles of pure deceit
You and I have found our lips can meet.

You and I have laughed the leagues apart
In the soft delight of heart to heart.

If there's a gulf to meet or limit set,
You and I have never found it yet.

You and I have trod the backward way
To the happy heart of yesterday,
To the love we felt in ages past
You and I have found it still to last.

You and I have found the joy had birth
In the angel childhood of the earth,
Hid within the heart of man and maid
You and I of Time are not afraid.

You and I can mock his fabled wing,
For a kiss is an immortal thing.
And the throb wherein those old lips met
Is a living music in us yet.

AE (George Russell)

Modern Love XXV

You like not that French novel? Tell me why.
You think it quite unnatural. Let us see.
The actors are, it seems, the usual three:
Husband, and wife, and lover. She – but fie!
In England we'll not hear of it. Edmond,
The lover, her devout chagrin doth share;
Blanc-mange and absinthe are his penitent fare,
Till his pale aspect makes her over-fond:
So, to preclude fresh sin, he tries rosbif.
Meantime the husband is no more abused:
Auguste forgives her ere the tear is used.
Then hangeth all on one tremendous IF: –
If she will choose between them. She does choose;
And takes her husband, like a proper wife.

Unnatural? My dear, these things are life:
And life, some think, is worthy of the Muse.

George Meredith

Mimnermus in Church

You promise heavens free from strife,
Pure truth, and perfect change of will;
But sweet, sweet is this human life,
So sweet, I fain would breathe it still;
Your chilly stars I can forgo,
This warm kind world is all I know.

You say there is no substance here,
One great reality above:
Back from that void I shrink in fear,
And child-like hide myself in love:
Show me what angels feel. Till then
I cling, a mere weak man, to men.

You bid me lift my mean desires
From faltering lips and fitful veins
To sexless souls, ideal quires,
Unwearied voices, wordless strains:
My mind with fonder welcome owns
One dear dead friend's remembered tones.

Forsooth the present we must give
To that which cannot pass away;
All beauteous things for which we live.
By laws of time and space decay.
But O, the very reason why
I clasp them, is because they die.

William Johnson Cory

A Clever Woman

You thought I had the strength of men,
Because with men I dared to speak,
And courted Science now and then,
And studied Latin for a week;
But woman's woman, even when
She reads her Ethics in the Greek.

You thought me wiser than my kind;
You thought me 'more than common tall';
You thought because I had a mind,
That I could have no heart at all;
But woman's woman you will find,
Whether she be great or small.

And then you needs must die – ah, well!
I knew you not, you loved not me.
'Twas not because that darkness fell,
You saw not what there was to see.
But I that saw and could not tell –
O evil Angel, set me free!

Mary E. Coleridge

An Oasis

You wandered in the desert waste, athirst;
My soul I gave you as a well to drink;
A little while you lingered at the brink,
And then you went, not either blessed or cursed.

The image of your face, which sank that day
Into the magic waters of the well,
Still haunts their clearness, still remains to tell
Of one who looked and drank and could not stay.

The sun shines down, the moon slants over it,
The stars look in and are reflected not;
Only your face, unchanged and unforgot,
Shines through the deep, till all the waves are lit.

My soul I gave you as a well to drink,
And in its depths your face is clearer far
Than any shine of sun or moon or star –
Since then you pause by many a greener brink.

A. Mary F. Robinson

Silent Noon

(From The House Of Life. Sonnet XIX)

Your hands lie open in the long fresh grass, –
The finger-points look through like rosy blooms:
Your eyes smile peace. The pasture gleams and glooms
'Neath billowing skies that scatter and amass.
All round our nest, far as the eye can pass,
Are golden kingcup-fields with silver edge
Where the cow-parsley skirts the hawthorn-hedge.
'Tis visible silence, still as the hour-glass.

Deep in the sun-searched growths the dragon-fly
Hangs like a blue thread loosened from the sky: –
So this wing'd hour is dropt to us from above.
Oh! clasp we to our hearts, for deathless dower,
This close-companioned inarticulate hour
When twofold silence was the song of love.

Dante Gabriel Rossetti

Leves Amores

Your kisses, and the way you curl
Delicious and distracting girl,
Into one's arms and round about
Inextricably in and out
Twining luxuriously, as twine
The clasping tangles of the vine;
So loving to be loved, so gay
And greedy for our holiday;
Strong to embrace and long to kiss
And strenuous for the sharper bliss,
A little tossing sea of sighs,
Till the slow calm seal up your eyes.
And then how prettily you sleep!
You nestle close and let me keep
My straying fingers in the nest
Of your warm comfortable breast;
And as I dream, lying awake,
Of sleep well wasted for your sake,
I feel the very pulse and heat
Of your young life-blood beat, and beat
With mine; and you are mine, my sweet!

Arthur Symons

Index of Poets and Poems

Index of Poems by Title

Index Of First Lines

I

T